VISUAL QUICKPRO GUIDE

DJANGO

Steven Holzner

Peachpit Press

Visual QuickPro Guide
Django
Steven Holzner

Peachpit Press

1249 Eighth Street
Berkeley, CA 94710
510/524-2178
510/524-2221 (fax)

Find us on the Web at: www.peachpit.com
To report errors, please send a note to: errata@peachpit.com
Peachpit Press is a division of Pearson Education.

Editor: Judy Ziajka
Production Coordinator: Myrna Vladic
Compositor: Debbie Roberti
Proofreader: Liz Welch
Indexer: Jack Lewis
Cover Design: Peachpit Press

ISBN 13: 978-0-321-64340-7
ISBN 10:   0-321-64340-2

9 8 7 6 5 4 3 2 1

Printed and bound in the United States of America

Dedication

To Nancy, of course!

Acknowledgments

The book you hold in your hands is the product of many people's work. I would particularly like to thank Wendy Sharp and Judy Ziajka for their tireless efforts to make this book the best it can be and Ed Tittel for his careful technical review of the entire manuscript.

TABLE OF CONTENTS

Chapter 8: Getting User Input: Django Forms   137

Chapter 9: Validating Form Data   157

Chapter 10: Logging Users In and Out   177

Index   195

INTRODUCTION

Welcome to the Django application framework. Django gives you a great deal of power by letting you create structured Web applications. When you create a Django application, Django creates the parts for you—you just fill in the blanks.

Of course, knowing what blanks to fill in takes some time, and knowing what to put in those blanks also takes some time. And that's where this book comes in.

You'll get a guided tour of Django applications here. You'll see how to create a basic application, use templates to create Web pages, display controls such as buttons and text fields in forms, style Django pages with CSS, log users in and out—and more.

What's in This Book

You'll start by seeing how to create Django projects and basic applications. Half the battle of getting used to working with Django is knowing what goes into what file, and this book covers that in depth.

Next, you'll learn the details of connecting Django applications to databases. An application is usually connected to a database, called the model. Creating this connection is easy, because you can use the database that comes built into Python.

Then you'll see how to connect the controlling part of the application, called the view in Django, to the database—that is, the model. Connecting the view to the model is an essential part of creating applications; when you have some data, you can store it in the model to persist after the user leaves, and the view lets you access that data when you want it.

You'll also learn to work with another important part of the Django equation at work: templates. Templates let you create skeletal Web pages for which the view can supply data. That's the way Django works: the view fetches data from the model, processes it, and sends it to a template so that data can appear in a Web page. In addition, you'll see how to make one template inherit Web page content from another.

This book also shows you how to use controls such as buttons and text fields in Web forms. You'll see how Django lets you create forms, display them, and access the data the user entered in them.

When you get data from the user, you can process and save that data in the model. You'll see how to create new data records and store them in the model.

You'll also see how to attach CSS files to Web pages in Django so you can style those pages.

Finally, you'll see how Django lets you log users in and out. You'll learn how to create log-in and log-out pages and let every page in between know whether the user is logged in.

That's the game plan, then: to put Django to work and see it at its most impressive.

WHAT'S IN THIS BOOK

What You'll Need

You won't need much in this book besides a knowledge of Python and HTML plus a Web browser.

You'll be able to download everything you need from the Internet: Python, the language Django uses, is free, as is Django itself. The database you'll use in this book comes with Python, as does a development server to let you test your applications. Chapter 1 shows you how to install all the necessary components.

Even if you're not an expert in Python, don't worry—the Python this book uses is pretty basic, and you'll be able to pick it up quickly if you know other programming languages. The thing to remember in Python that sometimes catches people by surprise is that indentation counts in Python code: you indent the code for functions, if statements, loops, and so on. If Python doesn't understand the way you've indented your code, it won't run that code. If you have any Python questions, just take a quick look at an online Python tutorial; that will be all you need.

That's it then—we're ready to start. We'll begin by installing Django in Chapter 1.

Getting Started: Installing Django

Django is a powerful Web application framework that lets you develop and deploy structured Web applications. That is to say, Django provides a framework in which to build Web apps. It's an advanced framework, providing everything you need to create extensive, scalable Web applications. The Django framework is written in the Python programming language, and it lets you program your application in Python.

With Django, you can build just about any Web site that it's possible to build. You can build an Internet shoe store, an auction site, a legal database, a language translation service, or just about anything else. Django specializes in sites that need database access—such as online store sites, or lookup sites for research, or blog sites—because Django interfaces well with databases on the server. In fact, Django stores the data it needs in a database, so you have to provide database access to get anywhere in Django.

This, our first Django chapter, provides a quick overview of what goes into a Django application.

You can build a Django project with a single command in Django, because Django takes care of the details for you. Within a project, you can create various applications— you can also create an empty application with a single command—and applications are what actually display pages on your site and interact with the user.

Each Django application is highly structured, and is created with placeholder files to which you add your own code. The structure reflects the modern model/view/controller (MVC) structure of Web applications.

continues on next page

In the standard MVC structure, the model is where you store and manage your data (the model can interact with your database), the view is what interacts with the user through Web pages, and the controller is the brains of the application, sending and getting data to and from the view and model and crunching that data to make the application actually do its thing.

Django, however, twists the standard structure a little. In Django, the model is still the model, but the view becomes the *template*, and the controller becomes, believe it or not, the *view*. So instead of a model/view/controller structure, Django applications have a model/template/view structure, which can take a little getting used to if you're an accomplished MVC programmer.

The Django Web site is at www.djangoproject.com, and that's where we'll grab Django—this book uses version 1.1. We'll also get Python and install it, although if you're not running Windows, there's a good chance you have Python already. This chapter takes you through the installation process for Django, and by the end of the chapter, you'll have Django up and running. You'll also create a first empty project (not an application yet) and see the default Django page in a browser.

Installing Python in Microsoft Windows

Django is a Python Web framework, so you'll need Python. Some operating systems come with Python installed, but not Windows, so unless you've installed Python already (or are using a different operating system), you need to install it now.

Django works with Python 2.3 to 2.6, but not yet with the experimental Python version 3, so we'll install version 2.6 for this book.

To install Python in Windows:

1. Navigate your browser to http://www.python.org/download.

2. Click the Windows installer link.

3. Click the Save button in the dialog box. A browse window opens.

4. Save the Windows installer .msi file on your hard disk in a subdirectory of your choice.

5. In Windows Explorer, double-click the installer .msi file.

6. Follow the directions the installer provides to install Python.

   For simplicity, we will install Python in a directory named python26 (accessible as c:\python26 in Windows) in this book, and it would be simplest if you do the same, modifying the last two digits to reflect the version of Python you're installing (by default, the installer places Python in the directory Python*XX*, where *XX* is the Python version number).

   There's no need to customize the Python setup, so you can accept the default configuration.

   continues on next page

You can also add Python to the Windows path, which makes Python simpler to use, although this step is not necessary for this book (if you add Python to the path, you can run it as c:\python instead of c:\python26\ python from the command prompt).

To add Python to the Windows path:

1. Open the Windows Control Panel.

2. Double-click the System icon.

3. Click the Advanced tab.

4. Click the Environment Variables button. The Environment Variables dialog box opens.

5. Append the directory in which you installed Python (for example, c:\python26) to the Path variable, separating it from the other paths with a semicolon.

6. Close the Environment Variables dialog box.

7. Close the System dialog box.

✔ Tips

- We'll test the Python installation later in this chapter.

- In Windows 7, the Advanced tab is called Advanced System Settings.

Installing Python in Linux or UNIX

If you have Linux or UNIX, the odds are good that you already have Python and so don't need to install. You can easily check to see whether you already have Python. If you don't have it, you'll need to install it.

To check whether you have Python in Linux or UNIX:

1. Open a terminal window.

2. At the command prompt, enter **python -V**.

   If you get a response like this (where $ is a placeholder for your system's command prompt), you already have Python installed:

   ```
   % python -V
   Python 2.6.1
   ```

   The version number for your copy of Python can differ, but make sure it is 2.3 or higher, but less than 3.0. If it is, you don't need to install Python.

   If you do need to install Python, follow the next steps.

To install Python in UNIX and API-based Linux systems:

1. If you have UNIX or an API-based Linux system such as Denebian or Ubuntu, you should use the system package manager, so open a terminal window.

2. Enter (where $ is a placeholder for your system command prompt):

   ```
   $ sudo apt-get update
   ```

3. Enter:

   ```
   $ sudo apt-get install python
   ```

4. Follow the displayed instructions.

5. Close the terminal window.

To install Python in Linux systems with the Synaptic package manager:

1. Open the Synaptic package manager.

2. Type **Python** in the search box and press **Enter**.

3. Select the Python package you want to install.

4. Click Apply.

5. Follow any directions from the package manager.

6. Close the package manager.

If you have any other Linux system, check your system's documentation to determine how to install or update Python if you need it.

INSTALLING PYTHON IN LINUX OR UNIX

Installing Python in Mac OS X

If you have Mac OS X, you already have Python, because Python comes with that operating system. However, if you have a version of Python before 2.3, you should update it.

You can easily check to see whether you already have an appropriate version of Python. If you don't, you can easily update it.

To check whether you have Python in Mac OS X:

1. Open a terminal window.

2. At the command prompt, enter **python -V**.

You should get a response like this (where $ is a placeholder for your system's command prompt):

```
% python -V
Python 2.6.1
```

If the version number for your copy of Python is 2.3 or higher, but less than 3.0, you don't need to install a new version of Python.

If you need to install a new version of Python, follow the next steps.

To install Python in Mac OS X:

1. Navigate your browser to http://www.python.org/download.

2. Click the Mac installer link.

3. Click the Save button in the dialog box.
   A browse window opens.

4. Save the Mac installer .dmg file on your hard disk in a subdirectory of your choice.

5. Double-click the installer .dmg file.

6. Follow the directions the installer provides to install Python.

   For simplicity, we will install Python in a directory named python26 in this book, and it would be simplest if you do the same, modifying the last two digits to reflect the version of Python you're installing (by default, the installer places Python in the directory Python*XX*, where *XX* is the Python version number).

```
usage: python [option] ... [-c cmd | -m
      mod | file | -]
Options and arguments (and corresponding
      environment variables):
-B        : don't write .py[co] files on
            import; also PYTHONDONTWRITEBY
-c cmd    : program passed in as string
            (terminates option list)
-d        : debug output from parser; also
            PYTHONDEBUG=x
-E        : ignore PYTHON* environment
            variables (such as PYTHONPATH)
-h        : print this help message and exit
            (also --help)
-i        : inspect interactively after
            running script; forces a prompt
            if stdin does not appear to be a
            terminal; also PYTHONINSPE
-m mod    : run library module as a script
            (terminates option list)
-O        : optimize generated bytecode
            slightly; also PYTHONOPTIMIZE=x
-OO       : remove doc-strings in addition
            to the -O optimizations
-Q arg    : division options: -Qold
            (default), -Qwarn, -Qwarnall, -Qnew
-s        : don't add user site directory to
            sys.path; also PYTHONNOUSE
-S        : don't imply 'import site' on
            initialization
-t        : issue warnings about
            inconsistent tab usage (-tt:
            issue err
-u        : unbuffered binary stdout and
            stderr; also PYTHONUNBUFFERED=
            see man page for details on
            internal buffering relating to
-v        : verbose (trace import
            statements); also PYTHONVERBOSE=x
            can be supplied multiple times
            to increase verbosity
-V        : print the Python version number
            and exit (also --version)
-W arg    : warning control; arg is
            action:message:category:module:line
          .
          .
          .
```

Listing 1.1 Python help information.

Testing Your Python Installation

If you've installed Python following the directions in this chapter or just want to see whether your Python version is appropriate to Django, you can easily test Python.

To test your Python installation:

1. Open a terminal window (in Windows, click Start and then choose All Programs > Accessories > Command Prompt).

2. Enter (where $ is a placeholder for your system's command prompt):

   `$ python –h`

   In Windows, if you haven't added Python to your system's path, you must also enter the path of the directory in which you installed Python (change 26 to the version number of Python you installed):

   `c:\>c:\python26 python -h`

   When you press **Enter**, you should see the Python help information scrolling up the window (**Listing 1.1**).

   If you see this help information, Python is working.

3. To test your version of Python, enter:

   `$ python -V`

   In Windows, if you haven't added Python to your system's path, you must also enter the path of the directory in which you installed Python, (change 26 to the version number of Python you installed):

   `c:\>c:\python26 python -V`

   When you press **Enter**, you should see the version number of Python displayed, something like this:

   `$ python -V`

   `Python 2.6`

   Make sure your version of Python is greater than or equal to 2.3 and less than 3.0.

Removing Any Old Versions of Django

If you've never installed Django on your computer, you can skip this topic.

If, on the other hand, you've installed Django before and intend to follow the directions in the following topics to upgrade to a newer version, you first must uninstall the older version of Django on your system.

The good news is that if you've installed Django using the Django setup.py program (which is the method used in this chapter), uninstalling Django is easy (great news for Windows users: the Windows registry isn't involved).

To uninstall an earlier version of Django installed with setup.py:

1. Open your system's file management application (in Windows, this is the Windows Explorer; in Mac OS X, it's the Finder; and so on).

2. Locate the site-packages folder for your Python distribution. This is usually the python*XX*/lib/site-packages directory, where *XX* is the version number of your Python installation (such as python26/ lib/site-packages for Python 2.6).

3. Double-click the site-packages folder to open it and locate the django folder inside it.

If you cannot locate the django folder, open a command prompt and enter this command (where $ is a placeholder for your system's command prompt):

```
$ python -c "from distutils.
sysconfig import get_python_lib;
print get_python_lib()"
```

If you're using Windows and did not add Python to the system path, enter the following (replace c:\python26 with the directory in which you installed Python if it's different):

```
c:\>c:\python26\python -c "from
distutils.sysconfig import get_
python_lib; print get_python_lib()"
```

When you press **Enter**, the location of the django folder should be displayed.

4. Delete the django folder.

5. Close your file management application.

After you've deleted the django folder in your Python installation's site-packages folder, you've deleted the earlier version of Django, and you're ready to install the current version.

REMOVING ANY OLD VERSIONS OF DJANGO

Installing Django in Windows

Installing Django in Windows is easier than you might think. All it really involves is downloading the compressed Django file, extracting it, and running a setup program.

To install Django in Windows:

1. Navigate your browser to http://www. djangoproject.com/download (**Figure 1.1**).

2. In the Get the Latest Official Version section, click the link to the Django .tar.gz file. This file name has the format Django-$X.X$.tar.gz, where $X.X$ is the latest version number. For example, for Django 1.1, the file is Django-1.1.tar.gz. Save the .tar.gz file to your hard disk.

3. Uncompress the .tar.gz file to a directory on your hard disk, such as c:\django-$X.X$. In this book, we'll uncompress Django to c:\django\django-1.1, but you can use any directory of your choice.

4. Click the Start button and then choose Programs > Accessories > Command Prompt.

✔ Tip

- Django comes compressed in .tar.gz format, not yet in .zip format, which is the Windows standard. You may already have installed a program that extracts .tar.gz files—you can double-click the .tar.gz file and see if it opens. If you don't have such a program, you can download one for free. The program 7-zip is often recommended for uncompressing Django in Windows, and you can get 7-zip.exe at http://www.7-zip.org/download.html. Winzip also works.

5. In the Command Prompt window, change to the Django-*X.X*, directory. For example, if you've installed Django to c:\Django-*X.X*, enter this at the command prompt:

```
c:\>cd c\Django-X.X
```

6. Run the setup program by entering this command:

```
c:\Django-X.X>python setup.py install
```

In Windows, if you haven't added Python to your computer's path, include the path to Python like this:

```
c:\Django-X.X>c:\python26\python setup.py install
```

7. To test your installation of Django, enter these commands:

```
C:\Django\Django-X.X>cd django\bin
```

```
C:\Django\Django-X.X\django\bin>c:\python26\python django-admin.py --version
```

In Windows, if you haven't included Python in your path, enter:

```
C:\Django\Django-X.X>cd django\bin
```

```
C:\Django\Django-X.X\django\bin>python django-admin.py --version
```

You should see the version number of your Django installation.

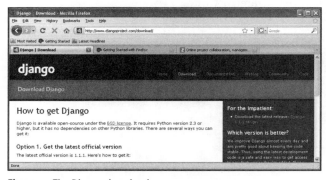

Figure 1.1 The Django download page.

Installing Django in Linux or UNIX and Mac OS X

Installing Django in Linux or UNIX and Mac OS X is not hard. All it really involves is downloading the compressed Django file, extracting it, and running a setup program.

The instructions presented next should work in all versions of Linux or UNIX and Mac OS X, but if you prefer to use your system's package manager (such as the one in Ubuntu), see the following task, "To install Django in Linux or UNIX and Mac OS X using a package manager."

To install Django in Linux or UNIX and Mac OS X:

1. Navigate your browser to http://www.djangoproject.com/download (see Figure 1.1 on the previous page).

2. In the Get the Latest Official Version section, click the link to the Django .tar.gz file. This file name has the format Django-*X.X*.tar.gz, where *X.X* is the latest version number. For example, for Django 1.1, the file is Django-1.1.tar.gz. Save the .tar.gz file to your hard disk.

3. Uncompress the .tar.gz file to a directory on your hard disk by entering this command in a command shell:

   ```
   $ tar xfz Django-X.X,tar.gz
   ```

4. Change to the Django-*X.X*, directory with this command:

   ```
   $ cd Django-X.X
   ```

5. Run the setup program by entering this command:

   ```
   $ sudo python setup.py install
   ```

6. To test your installation of Django, change directories as follows:

```
$ cd django\bin
```

7. Enter the following command:

```
$ django-admin.py --version
```

You should see the version number of your Django installation.

To install Django in Linux or UNIX and Mac OS X using a package manager:

1. In a command prompt window, enter this command:

```
$ sudo apt-get install python-django
```

2. To test your installation of Django, change directories as follows:

```
$ cd django\bin
```

3. Enter the following command:

```
$ django-admin.py --version
```

You should see the version number of your Django installation.

Installing a Database System

You can connect Django applications to Django's database application programming interface (API) if you set up a database system for use with Django. Django is frequently used with a database system, so we'll use a database system in this book.

If you've installed Python version 2.5 or later, you already have a database system—and in fact, it's the default one used by Django: SQLite. Because Django is built to easily connect to SQLite, we'll use SQLite in this book.

So if you have installed Python 2.5 or later and intend to use SQLite for your database system, you need not do anything more to install a database.

If you prefer to use a different database system, Django supports many systems. However, there's not usually much advantage in using a database system other than SQLite, because all database operations in Django are performed through the database API, which is a set of Python classes, which you use no matter what database system you have installed. So in terms of Django programming, there's no difference between SQLite and any other database system.

Django officially supports these database systems:

◆ PostgreSQL

◆ MySQL

◆ Oracle

◆ SQLite

In addition, backends provided by various software manufacturers allow you to use other databases with Django:

◆ Sybase SQL Anywhere

◆ IBM DB2

◆ Microsoft SQL Server 2005

◆ Firebird

◆ ODBC

If you want to use any of these database systems, make sure that the system is running before you develop your Django code (the exception is SQLite, which does not require a separate server).

Except with SQLite, you'll also need to make sure your database bindings are installed:

◆ If you're using PostgreSQL, you'll need the psycopg package. When you configure Django's database layer, you must specify either postgresql or postgresql_psycopg2.

◆ If you're using MySQL, you'll need MySQLdb version 1.2.1p2 or higher.

◆ If you're using SQLite and either Python 2.3 or 2.4, install pysqlite. Use version 2.0.3 or higher.

◆ If you're using Oracle, you'll need cx_Oracle.

We're also going to use Django's manage.py syncdb command to create tables in our databases, so make sure that Django has permission to create and edit tables in your database system (this step is not necessary with SQLite).

Creating an Empty Django Project

Now that you've installed Django, let's get it running.

Django lets you create projects, and in those projects, you create your individual applications. For example, we create a project in each chapter in this book—the project for this chapter is called chapter1—and starting in the next chapter, we create Web applications in each project.

When you create a project and synchronize the database system with your project, Django creates a default Web page that you can browse to. We'll create the project in the next task and set up the database in the following topic.

To create an empty Django project:

1. To create a Django project, you use the django-admin.py application, so open a command prompt and change to the directory that contains that application:

   `$ cd Django-1.1\django\bin`

   Note that you do not need to run django-admin.py from Django's bin directory. You can run this program from anywhere if you specify the path to it.

   If you copy django-admin.py to a directory in your system's path and have added Python to your system's path, you can run django-admin.py from any location just by typing its name at the command prompt.

   If you do copy django-admin.py to a directory in your system's path, you can actually delete the Django-1.1 folder, because it's not needed to create projects and applications (and Django has already been added to your Python installation).

2. Execute django-admin.py, telling it you want to start a new project named chapter1:

```
$ python django-admin.py
startproject chapter1
```

The django-admin.py program creates a new directory under the current directory named chapter1.

3. To verify that your new application's files exist, change to the chapter1 directory:

```
$ cd chapter1
```

4. Examine the new files in the chapter1 directory:

   ▲ In Windows, enter the command **dir**.

   ▲ In Linux or UNIX and Mac OS X, enter the command **ls -a**.

   You should see these newly created files:

   ▲ **manage.py**: This file is the project manager application. It lets you manage your project by performing such tasks as synchronizing the Django database system to the settings you plan to use in this project.

   ▲ **settings.py**: This file is where you record the settings you want for your project, such as the database system you want to use and the applications you have installed in your project.

   ▲ **urls.py**: This file lets you set up the URLs of the various applications in your project so that when someone enters a matching URL in a browser, the correct page from one of your application's appears.

   ▲ **__init__.py**: Django projects are actually Python packages, and this file tells Python that this folder contains a Python package.

To get your first project running, see the next task.

CREATING AN EMPTY DJANGO PROJECT

Setting Up the Database and Seeing a Django Page

In the previous task, you created a Django project named chapter1. Now we'll connect the database system (Django will use it to store its internal data) and launch the project's default Web page.

You can use Django with Web servers such as Apache, but how about getting some results right now, in this chapter? Django comes with a development Web server built right in, and we'll use that server here to launch our first Django page.

We'll set up the database using Python's built-in SQLite database system with the chapter1 project we created in the previous task.

To set up the database and see your Django project's page:

1. Using a text-editing program, open chapter1\settings.py and find the database section (**Listing 1.2**).

2. Enter **'sqlite3'** for the DATABASE_ENGINE setting and **'chapter1db'** for the DATABASE_NAME setting (**Listing 1.3**).

3. Save the file.

4. Open a command prompt, and in the chapter1 directory, enter this command to set up the database system:

   ```
   $ python manage.py syncdb
   ```

```
DATABASE_ENGINE = ''            #
       'postgresql_psycopg2',
       'postgresql', 'mysql', 'sqlite3'
       or 'oracle'.
DATABASE_NAME = ''              # Or path
       to database file if using
       sqlite3.
DATABASE_USER = ''              # Not used
       with sqlite3.
DATABASE_PASSWORD = ''          # Not used
       with sqlite3.
```

Listing 1.2 Editing settings.py.

```
DATABASE_ENGINE = 'sqlite3'     #
       'postgresql_psycopg2',
       'postgresql', 'mysql', 'sqlite3'
       or 'oracle'.
DATABASE_NAME = 'chapter1db'         # Or
       path
       to database file if using
       sqlite3.
DATABASE_USER = ''              # Not used
       with sqlite3.
DATABASE_PASSWORD = ''          # Not used
       with sqlite3.
```

Listing 1.3 The edited settings.py file.

5. When prompted to create a superuser for the database, respond as shown here:

You just installed Django's auth system, which means you don't have any superusers defined.

Would you like to create one now? (yes/no):

Enter **yes**.

Username:

Enter a name.

E-mail address:

Enter an email address.

Password:

Enter a password.

Password (again):

Enter the password again.

6. Start the Django development server by entering this command at the command prompt:

`$ python manage.py runserver`

7. Navigate your browser to http://localhost:8000/, and you should see the Django success page (**Figure 1.2**). Congratulations! Django is working.

8. Press **Ctrl+C** (Windows) or **Command+ Break** (Mac OS) to stop the server.

✔ Tip

- The Django development server runs on port 8000, but you can make it run on any port (8080 is the default for Web servers) by specifying that port as `$ python manage.py runserver xxxx`, where *xxxx* is the port number.

Figure 1.2 Our first Django page.

CREATING YOUR FIRST DJANGO APPLICATION

2

This is the chapter where it all starts. In this chapter, you're going to see how to create working Django applications.

When you create a project, as we did in the previous chapter, it's empty. You have to add your own applications to it, and that takes some work. We'll look at that here.

Next, you create a view for the application. The view is what's called the controller in MVC applications—it's the brain of the application. In this chapter, we'll create a view and link it to the application, a process that includes telling Django which URLs the user can enter to see your new view.

After creating the view and linking it to a URL, we'll launch the new application to make sure it actually runs. If everything looks good, we'll be underway.

Next, we'll change the view a little, to see what Django has in the way of data-handling power in the view. We'll define our own data in the view and make sure that this data appears in the browser.

After that, we'll modify the view still more to pass data to a Django template. Up to this point, our simple applications have been using the view to create the HTML that the user sees in the browser, but that's really the job of the template. A template (paradoxically called the view in standard MVC applications) is used to create the actual Web page that the user sees.

So we'll turn the view into a data handler, and it will pass its data to the template so the user can see that data. In the next chapter, you'll see how to set up a model for the application as well, and it's the model's job to store and make that data available to the view.

Let's get started creating our first Django app.

Creating the Project

The first step in getting a Django application running is to create a Django project.

Django applications live inside Django projects, so you'll need a project to start. The name of the project we create in this chapter is chapter2.

After creating the project and synchronizing the database to Django itself (so Django can use the database for its own internal data), we'll test the project briefly with the development server. If everything looks good, we'll add a new application to the project.

To create the Django project:

1. To create a Django project, you use the django-admin.py application, so open a command prompt and change to the directory that contains that application:

   ```
   $ cd Django-1.1\django\bin
   ```

2. Run django-admin.py, telling it you want to start a new project named chapter2:

   ```
   $ python django-admin.py
   startproject chapter2
   ```

   If you're using Microsoft Windows and haven't added Python to your system path, don't forget to give the path to Python as well:

   ```
   c:\>c:\python25\python django-admin.py
   startproject chapter2
   ```

   The django-admin.py program creates a new directory under the current directory, named chapter2.

✔ Tip

- As mentioned in the previous chapter, you don't need to run django-admin.py from Django's bin directory. You can run this program from anywhere if you specify the path to it.

3. To verify that your new application's files exist, change to the chapter2 directory:

```
$ cd chapter2
```

4. Examine the new files:
- ▲ In Windows, enter the command **dir**.
- ▲ In Linux/ or UNIX and Mac OS X, enter the command **ls -a**.

You should see these newly created files:
- ▲ manage.py
- ▲ settings.py
- ▲ urls.py
- ▲ __init__.py

Great—you've created the chapter2 project.

To actually get an application working, you need to:

- ◆ Create the project
- ◆ Synchronize the database
- ◆ Create the application
- ◆ Set up the view

We'll continue in the next task by setting up the database.

Setting Up the Database and Testing the Project

You need to set up a database to get a Django project running, let alone an application.

To set up the database, you need to edit settings.py in the project's directory and synchronize the database with Django.

After we set up the database and synchronize it, we'll test the project with the development server.

To set up the database:

1. Using a text-editing program, open chapter2\settings.py and find the database section (**Listing 2.1**).

2. Enter **'sqlite3'** for the DATABASE_ENGINE setting and **'firstdb'** for the DATABASE_NAME setting (**Listing 2.2**).

3. Save the file.

4. Open a command prompt, and in the chapter2 directory, enter this command to set up the database system:

   ```
   $ python manage.py syncdb
   ```

```
DATABASE_ENGINE = ''            #
     'postgresql_psycopg2',
     'postgresql', 'mysql', 'sqlite3'
     or 'oracle'.
DATABASE_NAME = ''              # Or path
     to database file if using
     sqlite3.
DATABASE_USER = ''              # Not used
     with sqlite3.
DATABASE_PASSWORD = ''          # Not used
     with sqlite3.
```

Listing 2.1 The settings.py file.

```
DATABASE_ENGINE = 'sqlite3'     #
     'postgresql_psycopg2',
     'postgresql', 'mysql', 'sqlite3'
     or 'oracle'.
DATABASE_NAME = 'firstdb'       #
     Or path
     to database file if using
     sqlite3.
DATABASE_USER = ''              # Not used
     with sqlite3.
DATABASE_PASSWORD = ''          # Not used
     with sqlite3.
```

Listing 2.2 Editing settings.py.

5. When prompted to create a superuser for the database, enter this data:

You just installed Django's auth system, which means you don't have any superusers defined.

Would you like to create one now? (yes/no):

Enter **yes**.

Username:

Enter a name.

E-mail address:

Enter an email address.

Password:

Enter a password.

Password (again):

Enter the password again.

6. Start the Django development server by entering this command at the command prompt:

```
$ python manage.py runserver
```

7. Navigate your browser to http://localhost:8000/, and you should see the Django success page (**Figure 2.1**). Excellent—the project is set up.

8. Press **Ctrl+C** (Windows) or **Command+Break** (Mac OS) to stop the server.

Figure 2.1 Our Django project page.

Creating the Application

Now we're going to set up the application. We'll name this first application first.

To create an application, you use the manage.py program. Django will create an application framework for you, and it's up to you to fill in the details and to add the parts you want.

After creating our new application, we have to let Django know about it; we do that by editing the `INSTALLED_APPS` section of settings.py.

To create the application:

1. Change to the project's directory, which in this case is chapter2:

   `$ cd chapter2`

2. Run the manage.py program to create the new application named first:

   `$ python manage.py startapp first`

3. To verify that your new application's files exist, change to the first directory:

   `$ cd firstdir`

4. Examine the new files:

   In Windows, enter the command **dir**.

   In Linux or UNIX and Mac OS X, enter the command **ls -a**.

   You should see these newly created files:

   ▲ **models.py**: This file lets you specify the model for the application, which stores and manages your application's data.

   ▲ **tests.py**: This file provides a testing program for your new application.

   ▲ **views.py**: This file is the brains behind your new application. It is where you define the code that runs when the user accesses your application.

   ▲ **__init__.py**: The program in this file tells Python that this directory contains a Python package.

```
INSTALLED_APPS = (
    'django.contrib.auth',
    'django.contrib.contenttypes',
    'django.contrib.sessions',
    'django.contrib.sites',
)
```

Listing 2.3 The settings.py file.

```
INSTALLED_APPS = (
    'django.contrib.auth',
    'django.contrib.contenttypes',
    'django.contrib.sessions',
    'django.contrib.sites',
    'chapter2.first',)
```

Listing 2.4 The edited settings.py file.

5. Now you have to tell Django about your new application. Open settings.py in the chapter2 project's directory and find the INSTALLED_APPS section (**Listing 2.3**).

6. Add this line to tell Django about the chapter2.first application (**Listing 2.4**).

7. Save the file.

Creating the Main View

Now we need to create the code that will run when a user accesses our application via a browser.

The main code for Web pages is in the view in Django. To create a view, you create a function in the file views.py.

For example, to create the view corresponding to the application's main page, you set up a function, which in this case we'll name main_page().

You use code in the view to pass Django the content it should pass to the browser. In this first example, we'll pass a simple HTML Web page to the browser.

After you set up the view, you have to link a URL to it; we'll do that in the next task before running and testing this application.

To create the main view:

1. Use a text editor (such as Microsoft WordPad) to open your application's views.py file.

    In this case, that file is chapter2\first\ views.py, and it currently contains the placeholder text shown in **Listing 2.5**.

2. Edit views.py to create a new function named main_page(), and import django. http import HttpResponse so that we can configure the response to the browser (**Listing 2.6**).

3. Edit views.py to create an output string with the HTML content we want to send to the browser, and pass that string to the browser using the HttpResponse() function (**Listing 2.7**).

4. Save the file.

✔ Tip

■ In Python, code indentation counts, so be sure to indent properly.

```
# Create your views here.
```

Listing 2.5 The default views.py file.

```
from django.http import HttpResponse

def main_page(request):
```

Listing 2.6 Adding a subroutine.

```
from django.http import HttpResponse

def main_page(request):
  output = '''
    <html>
      <head>
        <title>
          Our first application
        </title>
      </head>
      <body>
        <h1>
          Our first application
        </h1>
        Welcome to your first Django
          application.
      </body>
    </html>'''
  return HttpResponse(output)
```

Listing 2.7 Passing HTML content to the browser.

```
from django.conf.urls.defaults import *

# Uncomment the next two lines to
    enable the admin:
# from django.contrib import admin
# admin.autodiscover()

urlpatterns = patterns('',
    # Example:
    # (r'^chapter2/',
        include('chapter2.foo.urls')),

    # Uncomment the admin/doc line
        below and add
        'django.contrib.admindocs'
    # to INSTALLED_APPS to enable admin
        documentation:
    # (r'^admin/doc/',
        include('django.contrib.admindocs
        .urls')),

    # Uncomment the next line to enable
        the admin:
    # (r'^admin/',
        include(admin.site.urls)),
```

Listing 2.8 The default urls.py file.

```
from django.conf.urls.defaults import *
from first.views import *

# Uncomment the next two lines to
    enable the admin:
# from django.contrib import admin
# admin.autodiscover()

urlpatterns = patterns('',
    (r'^$', main_page),
)
```

Listing 2.9 The edited urls.py file.

Linking the View's URL to the Application

At this point, we've set up the view. We still have to tell Django when to display that view—that is, to what URLs that the user enters in the browser should the view respond?

You link a view to an actual URL in the project's urls.py file. You use standard regular expressions to specify the URL to match.

You link a URL's regular expression to a function defining that view in urls.py. In this case, we'll link all URLs entered in a browser connected to the development server to display the main_page view.

To link a view to a URL:

1. Use a text editor (such as Microsoft WordPad) to open the urls.py file in the project's directory—chapter2\urls.py in this case.

    You should see the code shown in **Listing 2.8**.

2. Edit urls.py so that it appears as shown in **Listing 2.9**, connecting the regular expression '^$' (which matches any single line of text—and therefore any URL) and connecting that URL to the main_page() function (which is contained in the main_page() function in views.py).

3. Save the file.

✔ Tip

■ For more on regular expression patterns, see http://docs.python.org/lib/module-re.html.

Launching Your First Application

The big moment has arrived: it's time to launch your first application.

This first application will display the Web page that we created in views.py, in the `main_page()` function (**Listing 2.10**).

Listing 2.10 shows the Web page we want to see: just a simple greeting, showing that the application is working.

To launch your first application:

1. Open a command prompt window.

2. Change to the project directory by entering a command something like this at the command prompt:

   `$ cd django-1.1\django\bin\chapter2`

3. Start the development server using manage.py:

   `$ python manage.py runserver`

   If you're using Windows and haven't added Python to the Windows path, don't forget to specify the path to Python by entering something like this:

   `c:\django-1.1\django\bin\`
   `chapter2>c:\python26\python`
   `manage.py runserver`

   This entry starts the Django test server on port 8000. If you want to start it on a different port, you have that option. For example, to start it on port 8080 (the normal port for Web servers), you would enter:

   `$ python manage.py runserver 8080`

```
<html>
  <head>
    <title>
      Our first application
    </title>
  </head>
  <body>
    <h1>
      Our first application
    </h1>
    Welcome to your first Django
      application.
  </body>
</html>
```

Listing 2.10 Our first Web page.

4. Navigate your browser to http://localhost:8000.

You should see the results shown in **Figure 2.2**, with the application started, and our Web page displayed in the browser.

Congratulations—you're running your first application.

Figure 2.2 Running our first application.

Defining a Template Directory

In Django, the view doesn't normally produce the actual HTML that gets displayed in the browser, as it has so far in this chapter. (In standard MVC frameworks, the view, as its name implies, is indeed the component that provides the HTML that is sent back to the browser.)

Instead, in Django applications, the actual rendering of the Web page, including creation of the HTML, is the job of the template.

So far, we've made the view send HTML back to the browser to keep things simple, but now that our first application is running, we will add a template to it to handle the actual HTML creation.

We'll store our templates in a directory named templates, and we'll need to inform Django that it should look in that directory for templates. That's the focus of this task: creating the templates directory and linking it to our first application, in preparation for adding a template to our application.

When we do add a template to our application, you'll see how to pass data from the view to the template for rendering—a standard task in Django applications.

To define a template directory:

1. Open a command prompt window.

2. Change to the project directory, which in this chapter is the chapter2 directory:

```
$ cd django-1.1\django\bin\chapter2
```

```
TEMPLATE_DIRS = (
    # Put strings here, like
        "/home/html/django_templates" or
        "C:/www/django/templates".
    # Always use forward slashes, even
        on Windows.
    # Don't forget to use absolute
        paths,
        not relative paths.
)
```

Listing 2.11 The settings.py template section.

```
TEMPLATE_DIRS = (
    # Put strings here, like
        "/home/html/django_templates" or
        "C:/www/django/templates".
    # Always use forward slashes, even
        on Windows.
    # Don't forget to use absolute
        paths,  not relative paths.
        "C:/Django-
        1.1/django/bin/chapter2/templates
        "
)
```

Listing 2.12 The current TEMPLATE_DIRS section.

3. Create the new templates directory:

`$ md templates`

Now we have a new directory named templates in the chapter2 directory (in addition to the first directory, which contains our first application).

Next we will tell Django that it should search in the templates directory for templates.

4. Using a text editor, open settings.py in the project's directory (chapter2) and locate the TEMPLATE_DIRS section (**Listing 2.11**).

5. Add the absolute path to your templates directory to the TEMPLATE_DIRS section (**Listing 2.12**):

- ▲ If you're using Linux or UNIX, the path might be something like: /home/django-1.1/django/bin/ chapter2/templates.

- ▲ If you're using Windows, the path might be something like this: C:/django-1.1/django/bin/ chapter2/templates.

6. Save the file.

✔ Tips

- ■ Windows users should use / as a path separator, not \.

- ■ Although the path shown here spans several lines to fit onto the book page, you should enter it all on one line in settings.py.

Passing Data to the Template

The view is the brains in a Django application. It fetches data from the model and crunches it and then tells the template what to display for the user in the browser.

Templates are typically HTML files, and the template we create in this chapter will display the application's main page, so we'll call our template main_page.html. To work with this template, the view needs to load the template, pass data to it, and then tell the template to render itself in the browser.

As we'll discuss in more detail in Chapter 4, "Connecting the View to the Model," you pass data to a template using a Django Context object. You load your variables into the Context object, pass that object to the template, and then tell the template to create the HTML that is sent to the browser.

To pass data to the template:

1. Open the application's views.py file, which is in the directory named first.

   Listing 2.13 shows the current contents of this file.

2. Edit the views.py file, making the changes shown in **Listing 2.14**.

   As will be discussed in more detail in Chapter 4, here we import the Context object so we can use it in our code to hold the data we pass to the template, and we import the get_template() function, which we use to load the template. We then configure the Context object with the variables we want—corresponding to the Web page's header, title, and body—and pass these variables to the template, asking the template to render itself in a string named output, which is passed back to the browser via the HttpResponse() function.

3. Save the file.

Now we're passing the variables head_title, page_title, and page_body to the template.

```python
from django.http import HttpResponse


def main_page(request):
  output = '''
    <html>
      <head>
        <title>
          Our first application
        </title>
      </head>
      <body>
        <h1>
          Our first application
        </h1>
        Welcome to your first Django
          application.
      </body>
    </html>'''
  return HttpResponse(output)
```

Listing 2.13 The current views.py file.

```python
from django.http import HttpResponse
from django.template import Context
from django.template.loader import
    get_template


def main_page(request):
  template =
    get_template('main_page.html')
  variables = Context({
    'head_title': 'First Application',
    'page_title': 'Welcome to our first
    application',
    'page_body': 'This is our first
    application, pretty good, eh?'
    })
    output =
    template.render(variables)
  return HttpResponse(output)
```

Listing 2.14 The edited views.py file.

```
<html>
  <head>
    <title>

    </title>
  </head>
  <body>
    <h1>

    </h1>
    <p>

    </p>
  </body>
</html>
```

Listing 2.15 The HTML part of the template.

```
<html>
  <head>
    <title>
      {{ head_title }}
    </title>
  </head>
  <body>
    <h1>
      {{ page_title }}
    </h1>
    <p>
      {{ page_body }}
    </p>
  </body>
</html>
```

Listing 2.16 The completed template.

Creating the Template

At this point, the view is passing these variables to the template in our application:

◆ `head_title =: 'First Application',`

◆ `page_title =: 'Welcome to our first application',`

◆ `page_body = 'This is our first application, pretty good, eh?'`

How do you read the `head_title`, `page_title`, and `page_body` variables in the template and display their text?

You do that by writing the template as an HTML document and embedding references to the variables passed to the template in a Context object. You enclose each such reference in double curly braces: `{{ variable_name }}`. When Django sees such a reference, it replaces the reference with the value of the referenced variable.

Our template, as referred to in views.py, is named main_page.html. Let's create that file now.

To create the template:

1. Using a text editor, create the file main_page.html in the templates directory (which is in the chapter2 project directory).

2. Enter the HTML for the page as shown in **Listing 2.15**.

3. Add the references to the variables passed to the template from the view—`head_title`, `page_title`, and `page_body`—to the template (**Listing 2.16**).

4. Save the file.

Launching the Improved Application

In this chapter, we've created an application that passes data from the view to the template. **Listing 2.17** shows the template as it first appeared.

When Django substitutes the values of the variables in the template, we end up with the HTML page shown in **Listing 2.18**.

We will confirm our work by running the new version of the application.

To launch the improved application:

1. Open a command prompt.

2. Change to the project directory—here, the chapter2 directory:

   `$ cd django-1.1\django\bin\chapter2`

3. Launch the development server by entering this command at the command prompt:

   `$ python manage.py runserver`

4. Navigate to http://localhpost:8000 in your browser.

   You should see the page that appears in **Figure 2.3**.

Now you've seen how to pass data from the view to the template.

```
<html>
  <head>
    <title>
      {{ head_title }}
    </title>
  </head>
  <body>
    <h1>
      {{ page_title }}
    </h1>
    <p>
      {{ page_body }}
    </p>
  </body>
</html>
```

Listing 2.17 The template.

```
<html>
  <head>
    <title>
      First Application
    </title>
  </head>
  <body>
    <h1>
      Welcome to our first application
    </h1>
    <p>
      This is our first
        application, pretty good, eh?
    </p>
  </body>
</html>
```

Listing 2.18 The template with data substituted in it.

Figure 2.3 The improved first application.

STORING DATA IN YOUR MODEL

In the previous chapter, we created our first Django application and got it running. That application gave us some experience with the structure of a Django project and an application in the project.

In particular, we set up two of the three primary parts of a Django application: the view and the template. We created two views: one that simply passed a text string containing HTML to the browser, and one that passed variables to the template. The variables in question contained text strings corresponding to the resulting Web page's title, header, and text. The template we created and connected to the application read the data passed to it through the Context object. The template read variables by name and inserted the data they contained into the Web page.

There's a third part to most Django applications—the model—and that's what this chapter is all about.

The model is your application's data repository. Because most applications want their data to stick around between sessions with the user, that data is stored in a database. In this book, we'll use SQLite, the database system that is by far the one most commonly used with Django, because it is built into Python and you don't need to install any code extensions to use it. You begin storing your data by telling the model how you want your data structured, and you use Django to create the tables you want to use in the database.

In this chapter, we'll set up a sample model that will be the backbone of a Web application (to be further developed in the next chapter, when we add the view and template to the model) that will allow you to store a list of your favorite Web sites. Each site will be recorded with a hyperlink, so we'll construct a table of hyperlinks in the model. The application can have many users, so we'll store the users in a users table.

continues on next page

We'll then be able to create Hyperlink objects to store URLs and User objects to store users of the Web application. The main table of the model will be the favorite table, and each record in the favorite table will record a hyperlink and the user who stored that hyperlink. When a user wants to store a new favorite in the application, the application will simply create a new entry in the favorite table. In that entry, we'll store the user and the new hyperlink that the user wants to record as a favorite. (In the next chapter, you'll see how to display a list of favorites for each user simply by looking up the appropriate favorites in the favorite table.)

That's the plan, then, for this chapter: to create a model that includes a table of hyperlinks and a table of users and also a table of favorites, each record of which stores a hyperlink and the user to whose favorite site the hyperlink corresponds. Our new application, which we'll call favorites, thus lets us store the URLs of favorite Web sites by user. Each stored favorite will have both a hyperlink and the name of the user who created the favorite.

We'll get started by creating the new project, chapter3, and the application in that project, favorites.

Creating the Project

The first step in getting any Django application working is to create a Django project. Following the naming convention in this book, the project for this chapter will be named chapter3.

After we create and test the chapter3 project, we'll add the new application, the favorites application, to it.

To create the Django project:

1. To create a Django project, you use the django-admin.py application, so open a command prompt and change to the directory that contains that application:

   ```
   $ cd Django-1.1\django\bin
   ```

2. Run django-admin.py, telling it you want to start a new project named chapter3:

   ```
   $ python django-admin.py
   startproject chapter3
   ```

   The django-admin.py program creates a new directory named chapter3 under the current directory.

3. To verify that your new application's files exist, change to the chapter3 directory:

   ```
   $ cd chapter3
   ```

✔ Tip

■ As mentioned earlier, you don't need to run django-admin.py from Django's bin directory. You can run this program from anywhere if you specify the path to it.

continues on next page

4. Examine the new files:

▲ In Windows, enter the command **dir**.

▲ In Linux or UNIX and Mac OS X, enter the command **ls -a**.

You should see these newly created files:

▲ manage.py

▲ settings.py

▲ urls.py

▲ __init__.py

The manage.py program lets you perform administrative tasks such as synchronizing the database and running the development server. The settings.py program lets you connect an application to the project (in the INSTALLED_APPS section) and set up the database for the project (in the DATABASE_NAME and DATABASE_ENGINE sections), and the urls.py program lets you connect a view to a URL that the user enters in the browser.

In this chapter, we'll use manage.py and settings.py; we'll use urls.py in the next chapter, when we connect the view and template to the application, not just the model.

Great—now we have a framework in which to create our favorites application. In the next task, we'll set up the database.

Setting Up the Database

To get a Django project working, you need to set up a database, and we'll do that in this task. We'll use SQLite for our database system, and edit settings.py to let Django know that we're using SQLite. We'll also specify a name for the database: favoritesdb.

To set up the database:

1. Using a text-editing program, open chapter3\settings.py and find the database section (**Listing 3.1**).

2. Enter `'sqlite3'` for the DATABASE_ ENGINE setting and **favoritesdb** for the DATABASE_NAME setting (**Listing 3.2**).

3. Save the file.

4. Open a command prompt and in the chapter3 directory, enter this command to set up the database system:

   `$ python manage.py syncdb`

5. When prompted to create a superuser for the database, enter this data:

   You just installed Django's auth system, which means you don't have any superusers defined.

   Would you like to create one now? (yes/no):

   Enter **yes**.

   Username:

   Enter a name.

   E-mail address:

   Enter an email address.

   Password:

   Enter a password.

   Password (again):

   Enter the password again.

continues on next page

```
DATABASE_ENGINE = ''          #
     'postgresql_psycopg2',
     'postgresql', 'mysql', 'sqlite3'
     or 'oracle'.
DATABASE_NAME = ''            # Or path
     to database file if using
     sqlite3.
DATABASE_USER = ''            # Not used
     with sqlite3.
DATABASE_PASSWORD = ''        # Not used
     with sqlite3.
```

Listing 3.1 The settings.py file.

```
DATABASE_ENGINE = 'sqlite3'       #
     'postgresql_psycopg2',
     'postgresql', 'mysql', 'sqlite3'
     or 'oracle'.
DATABASE_NAME = 'favoritesdb'        #
     Or path
     to database file if using
     sqlite3.
DATABASE_USER = ''            # Not used
     with sqlite3.
DATABASE_PASSWORD = ''        # Not used
     with sqlite3.
```

Listing 3.2 The edited settings.py file.

SETTING UP THE DATABASE

6. Start the Django development server by entering this command at the command prompt:

```
$ python manage.py runserver
```

7. Navigate your browser to http://localhost:8000/, and you should see the Django success page (**Figure 3.1**). Excellent—the project is set up.

8. Press **Ctrl+C** (Windows) or **Command+Break** (Mac OS) to stop the server.

Figure 3.1 Our Django project page.

```
INSTALLED_APPS = (
    'django.contrib.auth',
    'django.contrib.contenttypes',
    'django.contrib.sessions',
    'django.contrib.sites',
)
```

Listing 3.3 The settings.py file.

```
INSTALLED_APPS = (
    'django.contrib.auth',
    'django.contrib.contenttypes',
    'django.contrib.sessions',
    'django.contrib.sites',
    'chapter3.favorites',)
```

Listing 3.4 The edited settings.py file.

Creating the Favorites Application

You're ready to set up the favorites application. You'll use manage.py to set up the application, and it will create a new directory, favorites, for this application.

To create the favorites application:

1. Change to the project's directory, which in this case is chapter3:

   `$ cd chapter3`

2. Run the manage.py program to create the new application named favorites:

   `$ python manage.py startapp favorites`

3. To verify that your new application's files exist, change to the favorites directory:

   `$ cd favorites`

4. Examine the new files:
   ▲ In Windows, enter the command **dir**.
   ▲ In Linux or UNIX and Mac OS X, enter the command **ls -a**.

   You should see these newly created files:
   ▲ models.py
   ▲ tests.py
   ▲ views.py
   ▲ __init__.py

   We'll be using models.py in this chapter.

5. Tell Django about your new application, favorites. Open settings.py in the chapter3 project's directory and find the INSTALLED_APPS section (**Listing 3.3**).

6. Add code to tell Django about the chapter3.favorites application (**Listing 3.4**).

7. Save the file.

Planning the Model

Now we're ready to start planning the parts of our model. The model stores the data from our application, and the main model in our application will be the Favorite model, which lets you store a favorite Web site.

Each favorite will store a Hyperlink object and a User object (the name of the user who recorded the favorite). So we have three models to create:

◆ Favorite

◆ User

◆ Hyperlink

Thus, to create a favorite, the program needs to create a Favorite object and place in it a Hyperlink object and a User object.

You create these three models by creating Python classes, one for each model: Favorite, User, and Hyperlink. For example, if you want to create a model named Name to store a person's first name and last name, here's how you might start creating the Name class (this code will go into models.py):

```
class Name
```

The data in each class is stored in fields, and the data types for the fields are already defined in Django. To make those data types accessible, you import django.db import models:

```
from django.db import models
class Name
```

Then you indicate that you're basing your new model on the models.Model class:

```
from django.db import models

class Name(models.Model):
```

Table 3.1

Common Predefined Fields	
FIELD	VALUE
DateTimeField	Date and time values
EmailField	Email values
FileField	File upload fields
FloatField	Floating-point numbers
IntegerField	An integer
TextField	Text strings
URLField	URLs

Now you're free to define the new fields in your model. For example, the Name model is designed to store a first name and a last name, so you'd create fields named first_name and last_name, like this:

```
class hyperlink(models.Model):
    first_name = models.TextField()
    last_name = models.TextField()
```

That creates the Name model (after you create this model, you have to synchronize the database to make Django create the corresponding database table). Here, you created the first_name and last_name fields, making them of the predefined type models.TextField. Other predefined fields are also available for you to use in your models. **Table 3.1** lists the most common predefined fields and the information they store.

After you create your model's class and synchronize the database, you need to stock your model with data. This book looks at two ways to do that: manually (using the Django data-handling shell) and programmatically (our favorites application will let you create new records stored in the model in coming chapters).

In the next task, we get started by actually creating the Hyperlink model, asking Django to create a table for it in the database, and then adding some data to the Hyperlink model.

PLANNING THE MODEL

Creating the Hyperlink Model

Our favorites application will include three models: Favorite, User, and Hyperlink. We'll start with Hyperlink, the easiest model to create.

To create this model, we'll edit models.py and then synchronize the database. That will create a new table for hyperlinks in the application's database. Then, in the next task, we'll add data to the hyperlink table.

To create the Hyperlink model:

1. Use a text editor (such as Microsoft WordPad) to open the models.py file in the application's directory—in this case, chapter3\favorites\models.py.

   You should see the code shown in **Listing 3.5**.

2. Add the code to models.py that will create the new Hyperlink class (which supports the Hyperlink model):

   ```
   from django.db import models
   class Hyperlink
   ```

3. Indicate that you're basing your new model on the models.Model class:

   ```
   from django.db import models
   class Hyperlink(models.Model):
   ```

4. Define the new field in your model. The Hyperlink model is designed to store a URL, so add a field named url (**Listing 3.6**).

✔ Tip

■ In Python, code indentation counts, so be sure to indent properly.

```
from django.db import models

# Create your models here.
```

Listing 3.5 The original models.py file.

```
from django.db import models

class Hyperlink(models.Model):
    url = models.URLField()
```

Listing 3.6 The edited models.py file.

5. Save the file.

6. Open a command prompt.

7. Change to the project directory, which is chapter3 in this case, by entering code something like this (depending on where you created the project):

```
$ cd django-1.1\django\bin\chapter3
```

8. Synchronize the database, which means creating the tables your project needs if they don't already exist:

```
$ python manage.py syncdb
```

You should see:

```
$ python manage.py syncdb
Creating table favorites_hyperlink
```

Django created a new database table named favorites_hyperlink.

9. To verify the creation of the new table in the database, you can examine the actual SQL query that Django used to create the table. Enter this command at the command prompt:

```
$ python manage.py sql favorites
You should see:
BEGIN;
CREATE TABLE "favorites_hyperlink" (
    "id" integer NOT NULL PRIMARY KEY,
    "url" varchar(200) NOT NULL
);
COMMIT;
```

In other words, Django created two fields in our new table: "id" (ID fields are created automatically to let you access the records in the table) and "url", which is what we asked for.

At this point, the new model, Hyperlink, has been created. The next step is to add data to it.

Adding Hyperlink Data

We've created the Hyperlink model; now we'll add some data to the database by creating some Hyperlink objects.

To do that in this chapter, we'll use the Django data shell, which is an interactive window into your database.

To use the shell, you just start it with manage.py. Then you can issue commands that create new objects and examine existing ones. We'll use the shell here to create two new Hyperlink objects and save them in our database.

In future chapters, you'll see how to let your applications make changes to the database instead of having to make such changes manually.

To create Hyperlink objects:

1. Open a command prompt window.

2. Change to the project directory by entering code something like this at the command prompt:

   ```
   $ cd django-1.1\django\bin\chapter3
   ```

3. Start the Django data shell with manage.py:

   ```
   $ python manage.py shell
   ```

   The shell responds with a triple chevron prompt:

   ```
   >>>
   ```

4. At the prompt, load the models used in our favorites application:

   ```
   >>> from favorites.models import *
   ```

   The shell will load the models and display another >>> prompt.

✔ Tip

- Simply creating new objects isn't enough. You also have to explicitly save them in the database.

5. Create a new Hyperlink object named hyperlink1:

```
>>> hyperlink1 =
Hyperlink(url='http://www.
usatoday.com')
```

6. To put the new Hyperlink object in the database, you must save it like this:

```
>>> hyperlink1.save()
```

7. Verify that the hyperlink1 Hyperlink object's URL has been recorded properly:

```
>>> hyperlink1.url
'http://www.usatoday.com'
```

Here we can see that the URL is the one we entered. Good.

8. Create a second Hyperlink object:

```
>>> hyperlink2 =
Hyperlink(url='http://www.cnn.com')
```

9. Save the second Hyperlink object:

```
>>> hyperlink2.save()
```

Now hyperlink1 is a Hyperlink object, and it was automatically given the ID 1, and hyperlink2 is a Hyperlink object and was automatically given the ID 2.

10. Verify that the hyperlink1 object has an ID of 1 by entering this command:

```
>>> Hyperlink.objects.get(id=1).url
```

The shell responds with the correct URL of hyperlink1, confirming that the hyperlink1 object has an ID of 1:

```
>>> Hyperlink.objects.get(id=1).url
'http://www.usatoday.com'
```

11. Exit the shell with the exit() command:

```
>>> exit()
```

12. Synchronize the database to make sure that any changes are recorded (theoretically, this step is not necessary, but it's a good idea in practice):

```
$ python manage.py syncdb
```

✔ **Tip**

■ You can access previously entered commands in the shell by pressing the Up arrow on your keyboard. When a previous command appears at the >>> prompt, you can edit it and then press **Enter** to run the edited command.

ADDING HYPERLINK DATA

Handling Data in the Shell

The Django shell, accessible through manage.py, gives you access to your data, and it pays to know how to use the shell.

There are many different ways of using the shell to access your data, and we'll look at some of them in this task. These methods will come in handy as you enter and edit the data in your applications, especially as your application data becomes more extensive and complex.

Setting up your data with the right structure is often half the battle of writing a Django application. The correct data structure can make your programming a snap, but the wrong data structure will fight you all the way.

Let's look at a few of the commands available in the shell.

To define a template directory:

1. Open a command prompt window.

2. Change to the project directory, which is the chapter3 directory in this chapter:

    ```
    $ cd django-1.1\django\bin\chapter3
    ```

3. Start the Django data shell with manage.py:

    ```
    $ python manage.py shell
    ```

    The shell responds with a triple chevron prompt:

    ```
    >>>
    ```

4. Load the models from your application. In this chapter, the application is named favorites, so that import command looks like this:

    ```
    >>> from favorites.models import *
    ```

5. To refer to the objects of a particular kind, enter the class name followed by **objects**. To count the number of Hyperlink objects, use this command:

```
>>> Hyperlink.objects.count()
```

The shell responds with the number of objects of that type:

```
>>> Hyperlink.objects.count()
2
```

In this case, the shell reports that you have two Hyperlink objects, which is correct.

6. To examine a field in an object, enter the object identifier followed by the field name. To find the URL of the Hyperlink object with the ID 2, use this command:

```
>>> Hyperlink.objects.get(id=2).url
```

The shell returns the value of the field you asked for:

```
>>> Hyperlink.objects.get(id=2).url
'http://www.cnn.com'
```

7. You can collect all Hyperlink objects into a collection named `hyperlinks` using this command:

```
>>> hyperlinks =
Hyperlink.objects.all()
```

8. You can loop over all members of the `hyperlinks` collection with these commands:

9. To delete an object, use the `delete()` command:

```
>>> Hyperlink.objects.get(id=2).
delete()
```

10. To save an object, use the `save()` command:

```
>>> hyperlink3.save()
```

11. To exit the shell, use the `exit()` command:

```
>>> exit()
```

✔ **Tip**

■ Note that the `print` command is indented, so be sure to add two spaces in front of it when entering it, because indentation counts in Python. The three dots (. . .) are printed by the shell.

```
>>> for hyperlink in hyperlinks:
...     print hyperlink.url
...
```

The shell responds with the URLs of the Hyperlink objects:

```
>>> for hyperlink in hyperlinks:
...     print hyperlink.url
...
http://www.usatoday.com
http://www.cnn.com
```

Creating the User Model

One of the three models we'll need is the User model, which will store the user's name and password.

So are we going to create a User model as we just created the Hyperlink model? Surprise! Django comes with a User model built in, so we won't need to create the User model at all.

In fact, we already have a user in our database: the superuser we created when we first synchronized the database. To verify this, start the shell:

```
$ python manage.py shell
```

At the shell prompt, import that User model, which is technically the `django.contrib.auth.models` User model:

```
>>> from django.contrib.auth.models import User
```

Now look at all existing User objects:

```
>>> User.objects.all()
[<User: steve>]
```

There's just one existing User object corresponding to Steve, the current superuser.

To see the fields and methods of User objects, you can use the `dir(User)` command:

```
>>> dir(User)
```

This command returns a listing of all the fields and methods of the User object (including fields and methods meant only for internal Django use):

```
>>> dir(User)
```

```
['DoesNotExist',
'MultipleObjectsReturned', '__class__',
'__delattr__', '__doc__', '__eq__',
'__format__', '__getattribute__',
'__hash__', '__metaclass__', '__
module__', '__ne__', '__new__',
'__reduce__',x__', '__repr__', '__
setattr__', '__sizeof__', '__str__',
'__subclas_unicode__', '__weakref__',
'_base_manager', '_collect_sub_
objects',
```

```
anager', '_deferred', get_FIELD_
display', '_get_next_or_previous_
bget_next_or_previous_in_order',
'_get_pk_val', '_meta', '_set_pk_val
ssword', 'date_joined', 'delete',
'email', 'email_user', 'first_name
lute_url', 'get_all_permissions',
'get_and_delete_messages', 'get_fu
```

```
et_group_permissions', 'get_next_by_
date_joined',          .
```

.

Table 3.2 lists the built-in fields of the User model.

Table 3.2

Built-in Fields of the User Model		
FIELD	REQUIRED OR OPTIONAL	VALUE
username	Required	30 characters or fewer; contains the username for the user
first_name	Optional	30 characters or fewer
last_name	Optional	30 characters or fewer
email	Optional	Email address
password	Required	Django doesn't actually store the password; it stores a hash corresponding to the password

To create the User model:

1. In the application directory, favorites, edit models.py and add the line shown in **Listing 3.7**.

2. Save the file.

3. At a command prompt, synchronize the database:

   ```
   $ python manage.py syncdb
   ```

```
from django.db import models
from django.contrib.auth.models import User

class Hyperlink(models.Model):
  url = models.URLField()
```

Listing 3.7 The models.py file.

Creating the Favorite Model

Our favorites application is meant to store favorite Web sites for users. Each favorite is stored in a Favorite object, and each Favorite object contains the name of the user whose favorite it is and a hyperlink to the Web site that the user wants to make a favorite—so the Favorite model will contain three fields:

◆ **title**: The title of the favorite (such as 'USA Today')

◆ **user**: The user whose favorite this is

◆ **hyperlink**: The link for the Web site that the user wants to record as a favorite

We'll start the Favorite model with the title field:

```
class Favorite(models.Model):
    title = models.CharField(max_
    length=200)
```

Here's the important part: rather than storing user and hyperlink data, we'll store only a reference to existing external User and Hyperlink objects. So you create a User object and a Hyperlink object first; then you store a reference to them in a Favorite object when it's time to record a favorite. You store references to external objects using the models. ForeignKey method:

```
class Favorite(models.Model):

    title =    models.CharField(max_
    length=200)

    user = models.ForeignKey(User)

    hyperlink =    models.
    ForeignKey(Hyperlink)
```

Now we're ready to create the Favorite model.

✔ Tip

■ For text fields, you have to specify the maximum length you want to allow.

To create the Favorite model:

1. Using a text editor, open models.py in the application directory (the chapter3\favorites directory here).

   Listing 3.8 shows the current version of models.py.

2. Add the code to define the Favorite model (**Listing 3.9**).

3. Save the file.

4. Open a command prompt, change to the application directory, and synchronize the database with this command:

   `$ python manage.py syncdb`

   You should get a response like this:

   ```
   $ python manage.py syncdb
   Creating table favorites_favorite
   Installing index for favorites.
   Favorite model
   ```

The Favorite model has been created. The next step is to add some data to it.

```
from django.db import models
from django.contrib.auth.models import User

class Hyperlink(models.Model):
  url = models.URLField()
```

Listing 3.8 The current models.py file.

```
from django.db import models
from django.contrib.auth.models import User

class Hyperlink(models.Model):
  url = models.URLField()

class Favorite(models.Model):
  title =
      models.CharField(max_length=200)
  user = models.ForeignKey(User)
  hyperlink =
      models.ForeignKey(Hyperlink)
```

Listing 3.9 The completed models.py file.

Adding Favorite Data

Now that we've created the Favorite model, we're going to add some data to it. We'll do that with the shell, accessing our database, which already contains Hyperlink and User objects that we'll use.

In particular, we've already defined two hyperlinks and have one user in our database. We'll put together a Favorite object that refers to the existing user and the first hyperlink (which points to 'USA Today').

After we create the Favorite object, we'll save it in the database. In the next chapter, we'll access the data in our database and display it.

To add Favorite data:

1. Open a command prompt.

2. Change to the project directory—here, that's the chapter3 directory:

   ```
   $ cd django-1.1\django\bin\chapter3
   ```

3. Start the shell:

   ```
   $ python manage.py shell
   ```

4. Load the User model in the shell:

   ```
   >>> from django.contrib.auth.models
   import User
   ```

5. Load the models for our application:

   ```
   >>> from favorites.models import *
   ```

6. We need a User object, so create one that corresponds to the existing User object with ID 1:

   ```
   >>> user = User.objects.get(id=1)
   ```

7. We also need a Hyperlink object, so create one corresponding to the existing Hyperlink object with ID 1:

   ```
   >>> hyperlink =
   Hyperlink.objects.get(id=1)
   ```

continues on next page

8. Start creating a new Favorite object:

```
>>> favorite = Favorite(
```

9. Add the fields of the Favorite object (indenting two spaces at the start of each one):

```
>>> favorite = Favorite(
...   title = 'USA Today',
...   user = user,
...   hyperlink = hyperlink
```

10. Finish the Favorite object with a closing parenthesis:

```
>>> favorite = Favorite(
...   title = 'USA Today',
...   user = user,
...   hyperlink = hyperlink
... )
```

11. Confirm the contents of the Favorite object by examining some of its fields:

```
>>> favorite.hyperlink.url
'http://www.usatoday.com'
>>> favorite.user.username
'steve'
```

12. Save the new Favorite object:

```
>>> favorite.save()
```

13. Exit the shell:

```
>>> exit()
```

And that's it: you've loaded the model with data. In the next chapter, we'll put that data to work.

CONNECTING THE VIEW TO THE MODEL

In the previous chapter, we created three models: Favorites, User, and Hyperlink. In this chapter, we'll put those models to work.

Specifically, our models were set up to let us record the favorite Web sites, by URL, of users. We can record a URL in the Hyperlink model and a user in the User model and then record both the user and the user's selected hyperlink in the Favorite model (from models.py, where you define your models in a Django application).

We created a Hyperlink model with one field, url:

```
class Hyperlink(models.Model):
  url = models.URLField()
```

The User model is built into Django, so all we had to do was import it, like this:

```
from django.contrib.auth.models import User
```

The Favorite model lets us store a user and a hyperlink—so, for example, if the user 'steve' listed USA Today as one of his favorite Web sites, we could record both the user and hyperlink in a Favorite object, which was defined like this in models.py:

```
class Favorite(models.Model):
  title =    models.CharField(max_length=200)
  user = models.ForeignKey(User)
  hyperlink =  models.ForeignKey(Hyperlink)
```

We set up the models in the previous chapter and filled the models with some data using the shell. In this chapter, we'll use those models, accessing the models from the view.

continues on next page

Does that mean that we have to create the models all over again and fill them with data a second time for the new chapter4 (as opposed to chapter3) project? Not at all. You can transfer databases between Django projects if you are careful about what you're doing, and you'll see how in this chapter.

After transferring the database, we'll access that database from the view in our new application: the favorites application in the chapter4 project. After all, the best model in the world is of no use to us if we can't access the data in that model.

So that's the plan in this chapter: create the chapter4 project, create the favorites application in it, transfer the database we created in the previous chapter, and then access the model's data from the new application's view (recall that in Django applications, the view is the brains of the application).

✔ Tip

■ Transferring the database also means transferring models.py, because when you synchronize the database, all tables not in models.py or used internally by Django are totally wiped out.

```
INSTALLED_APPS = (
    'django.contrib.auth',
    'django.contrib.contenttypes',
    'django.contrib.sessions',
    'django.contrib.sites',
)
```

Listing 4.1 The settings.py file.

Creating the Project and Application

The first step is to create the chapter4 project and then create the favorites application inside that project. That's what we'll do in this task.

To create the Django project and application:

1. To create the Django project, use django-admin.py. Open a command prompt and change to the directory that contains that application:

   `$ cd Django-1.1\django\bin`

   As discussed in previous chapters, you do not need to run django-admin.py from Django's bin directory. You can run this program from anywhere if you specify the path to it.

2. Run django-admin.py, telling it you want to start a new project named chapter4:

   `$ python django-admin.py`
   `    startproject chapter4`

   The django-admin.py program creates a new directory named chapter4 under the current directory.

3. Change to the chapter4 directory:

   `$ cd chapter4`

4. Run the manage.py program to create the new application named first like this:

   `$ python manage.py startapp favorites`

5. Now you have to tell Django about your new application, favorites. Open settings.py in the chapter4 project's directory and find the INSTALLED_APPS section (**Listing 4.1**).

continues on next page

CREATING THE PROJECT AND APPLICATION

6. Add a line to tell Django about the chapter4.favorites application, shown in **Listing 4.2**.

7. Save the file.

Now we have a new project, named chapter4, and a new application, named favorites. The next step is to transfer the database file, favoritesdb, that we created so carefully in the previous chapter.

```
INSTALLED_APPS = (
    'django.contrib.auth',
    'django.contrib.contenttypes',
    'django.contrib.sessions',
    'django.contrib.sites',
    'chapter4.favorites',)
```

Listing 4.2 The edited settings.py file.

```
DATABASE_ENGINE = ''          #
     'postgresql_psycopg2',
     'postgresql', 'mysql', 'sqlite3'
     or 'oracle'.
DATABASE_NAME = ''            # Or path
     to database file if using   sqlite3.
DATABASE_USER = ''            # Not used
     with sqlite3.
DATABASE_PASSWORD = ''        # Not used
     with sqlite3.
```

Listing 4.3 The settings.py file.

Transferring the Database

As mentioned at the beginning of the chapter, we created Hyperlink and Favorite models, and we created objects of each. Rather than repeat all that work, we'll copy the database file, favoritesdb, that was created in Chapter 3.

The copy process involves these steps:

◆ Copy favoritesdb.

◆ Copy models.py.

◆ Edit settings.py to create the database favoritesdb.

◆ Synchronize the database.

To transfer the database:

1. Copy the database, favoritesdb, from the chapter3 folder to the chapter4 folder.

   This is the big step, because the favoritesdb database contains the tables and data that we'll use in this chapter.

2. Copy models.py from chapter3\favorites to chapter4\favorites. (If your operating system asks whether you want to replace the existing models.py, answer Yes.)

   The models.py file contains the definition of the models you want to use. Unless you copy the version of models.py created in Chapter 3 that defines the models, you'll lose the models in the database when you synchronize the database.

3. Using a text-editing program, open chapter4\settings.py and find the database section (**Listing 4.3**).

continues on next page

4. Enter **'sqlite3'** for the DATABASE_ ENGINE setting and **favoritesdb** for the DATABASE_NAME setting (**Listing 4.4**).

5. Save the file.

6. Open a command prompt, and in the chapter4 directory, enter this command to set up the database system:

```
$ python manage.py syncdb
```

You will not be prompted to create a superuser account, since that account already exists in the chapter3 favoritesdb database.

Excellent—the database is set up, having been transferred from the chapter3 project.

```
DATABASE_ENGINE = 'sqlite3'          #
    'postgresql_psycopg2',
    'postgresql', 'mysql', 'sqlite3'
    or 'oracle'.
DATABASE_NAME = 'favoritesdb'        #
    Or path
    to database file if using
    sqlite3.
DATABASE_USER = ''              # Not used
    with sqlite3.
DATABASE_PASSWORD = ''          # Not used
    with sqlite3.
```

Listing 4.4 The edited settings.py file.

```
from django.http import HttpResponse

def main_page(request):
  output = '''
    <html>
      <head>
        <title>
          Connecting to the model
        </title>
      </head>
      <body>
        <h1>
          Connecting to the model
        </h1>
        We will use this application to
          connect to the model.
      </body>
    </html>'''
  return HttpResponse(output)
```

Listing 4.5 The edited views.py file.

```
from django.conf.urls.defaults import *
from favorites.views import *

# Uncomment the next two lines to enable
    the admin:
# from django.contrib import admin
# admin.autodiscover()

urlpatterns = patterns('',
  (r'^$', main_page),
)
```

Listing 4.6 The edited urls.py file.

Creating the View

The next task in getting our favorites application running is to create the view. That involves two steps: first, we have to write views.py, and second, we have to tell Django about the view we've set up by editing urls.py.

To create the view:

1. Using a text editor, edit chapter4\favorites\ views.py to add a new view named main_ page, replacing the current version of views.py with the code in **Listing 4.5**.

2. Save views.py.

3. Edit chapter4\urls.py to add the main_ page view to the application, making the additions shown in **Listing 4.6**.

4. Save urls.py.

5. Open a command prompt and navigate to the chapter4 directory:

    `$ cd django-1.1\django\bin\chapter4`

6. Run the development server:

    `$ python manage.py runserver`

7. Navigate your browser to http:// localhost:8000.

    You should see the Web page shown in **Figure 4.1**.

✔ Tip

■ In Python, code indentation counts, so be sure to indent properly.

    This version of views.py simply displays a placeholder Web page.

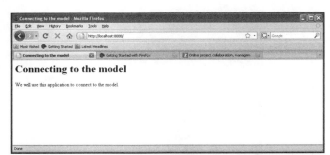

Figure 4.1 Starting our favorites application.

Displaying Data from the View

The previous task displayed a placeholder Web page, but no actual data. We need some way to display data in our Web pages, because the goal of this chapter is to fetch data from the model and display it.

Django provides a special syntax you can use to insert data into your Django Web pages in the view, and you'll see how that works in this task.

Here, we'll insert the text string "Here is the text!" into the Web page to see how inserting data from a view works.

To display data from the view:

1. Using a text editor, edit chapter4\
favorites\views.py, adding the code
shown in **Listing 4.7**.

   This code lets you include a list of data values in the parentheses after the **%** character that will be inserted into the earlier text. In this case, we're indicating that we're going to list one text string that should be inserted at the location of the **%s** code.

```
from django.http import HttpResponse

def main_page(request):
  output = '''
    <html>
      <head>
        <title>
          Connecting to the model
        </title>
      </head>
      <body>
        <h1>
          Connecting to the model
        </h1>
        %s
      </body>
    </html>''' % (
            .
            .
            .
    )
  return HttpResponse(output)
```

Listing 4.7 The edited views.py file.

```
from django.http import HttpResponse

def main_page(request):
  output = '''
    <html>
      <head>
        <title>
          Connecting to the model
        </title>
      </head>
      <body>
        <h1>
          Connecting to the model
        </h1>
        %s
      </body>
    </html>''' % (
      'Here is the text!'
    )
  return HttpResponse(output)
```

Listing 4.8 The completed views.py file.

2. Add the 'Here is the text!' text string that will be inserted into the Web page at the location of the %s code (**Listing 4.8**).

3. Save views.py.

4. Open a command prompt and navigate to the chapter4 directory:

   $ cd django-1.1\django\bin\chapter4

5. Run the development server:

   $ python manage.py runserver

6. Navigate your browser to http://localhost:8000.

   You should see the Web page shown in **Figure 4.2**.

Now you know how to insert data into a Web page created in the view. The next step is to fetch some data from the model and display it in the Web page, which we'll do in the following task.

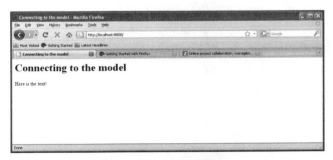

Figure 4.2 Displaying data inserted into a Web page.

Accessing the First Favorite from the Model

In this task, we'll begin accessing data from the model using code in the view. In particular, we'll access the first Favorite object, created in Chapter 3, and display its title in a Web page.

To do that, we have to make the code in the view aware of the model, and you do that by importing all the models from favorites.models (the compiled models.py) in views.py:

```
from favorites.models import *
```

Accessing the model in code works much as it did in the shell in Chapter 3. For example, to access the Favorite objects in the model, you use this syntax:

```
Favorite.objects
```

To get the first Favorite object, use the `get` method, getting the Favorite object with the ID of 1:

```
Favorite.objects.get(id=1)
```

Then to access the Favorite object's `title` field, use this syntax:

```
Favoite.objects.get(id=1).title
```

And that's how we'll access the title of the first favorite Web site in the database (you may recall from Chapter 3 that the title of the first favorite was USA Today).

To access the first favorite from the model:

1. Using a text editor, edit chapter4\favorites\views.py, adding the code shown in **Listing 4.9**.

```
from django.http import HttpResponse
from favorites.models import *


def main_page(request):
  output = '''
    <html>
      <head>
        <title>
          Connecting to the model
        </title>
      </head>
      <body>
        <h1>
          Connecting to the model
        </h1>
        Here's the title of the first
            favorite: %s
      </body>
    </html>''' % (
          .
          .
          .
    )
    return HttpResponse(output)
```

Listing 4.9 The edited views.py file.

```
from django.http import HttpResponse
from favorites.models import *
def main_page(request):
  title = Favorite.objects.get(id=1).title
  output = '''
   <html>
     <head>
       <title>
         Connecting to the model
       </title>
     </head>
     <body>
       <h1>
         Connecting to the model
       </h1>
       Here's the title of the first
           favorite: %s
     </body>
   </html>''' % (
       title
   )
  return HttpResponse(output)
```

Listing 4.10 The completed views.py file.

2. Add the code to actually access the title of the first favorite and display it, shown in **Listing 4.10**.

3. Save views.py.

4. Open a command prompt and navigate to the chapter4 directory:

   $ cd django-1.1\django\bin\chapter4

5. Run the development server:

   $ python manage.py runserver

6. Navigate your browser to http://localhost:8000.

   You should see the Web page shown in **Figure 4.3**.

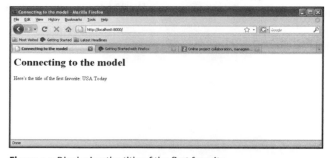

Figure 4.3 Displaying the title of the first favorite.

Accessing a Specific User

You can also access User objects in code. For example, you might want to access a user's email address, which is recorded in the User field email.

Using the get method, you can access a specific user by username. At this point, the database contains only one user: the superuser we created in the previous chapter. In the database shown in this book, that superuser is 'steve' (substitute your own superuser name to make this example work):

```
User.objects.get(username='steve')
```

Also, you can access the user's email address using the User object's email field:

```
email = User.objects.
    get(username='steve').email
```

Let's put this process to work in views.py.

To access a specific user:

1. Using a text editor, edit chapter4\favorites\views.py, adding the code shown in **Listing 4.11**.

```
from django.http import HttpResponse
from django.contrib.auth.models import User
from favorites.models import *

def main_page(request):
  output = '''
    <html>
      <head>
        <title>
          Connecting to the model
        </title>
      </head>
      <body>
        <h1>
          Connecting to the model
        </h1>
        User steve's email: %s
      </body>
    </html>''' % (
          .
          .
          .
    )
    return HttpResponse(output)
```

Listing 4.11 The edited views.py file.

```
from django.http import HttpResponse
from django.contrib.auth.models import User
from favorites.models import *

def main_page(request):
  email = User.objects.
get(username='steve').email
  output = '''
    <html>
      <head>
        <title>
          Connecting to the model
        </title>
      </head>
      <body>
        <h1>
          Connecting to the model
        </h1>
        User steve's email: %s
      </body>
    </html>''' % (
        email
    )
  return HttpResponse(output)
```

Listing 4.12 The completed views.py file.

2. Add the code to actually access the user's email and display it, shown in **Listing 4.12**.

3. Save views.py.

4. Open a command prompt and navigate to the chapter4 directory:

`$ cd django-1.1\django\bin\chapter4`

5. Run the development server:

`$ python manage.py runserver`

6. Navigate your browser to http:// localhost:8000.

You should see the Web page shown in **Figure 4.4**.

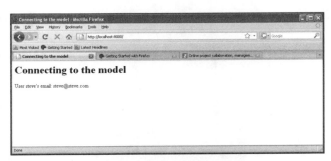

Figure 4.4 Displaying a user's email address.

Accessing a Specific User's Favorite

In this task, we'll display the title of a user's favorite. We'll start by getting an object corresponding to the user (change the name of the user as appropriate to match your database):

```
user = User.objects.
    get(username='steve')
```

Then, to find the title of the favorite, just pass the `get` method the User object to get the user's favorite, and use the `title` field to find the favorite's title:

```
user = User.objects.
    get(username='steve')

title = Favorite.objects.
    get(user=user).title
```

To access a specific user's favorite:

1. Using a text editor, edit chapter4\
   favorites\views.py, adding the code
   shown in **Listing 4.13**.

```
from django.http import HttpResponse
from django.contrib.auth.models import User
from favorites.models import *

def main_page(request):
  output = '''
    <html>
      <head>
        <title>
          Connecting to the model
        </title>
      </head>
      <body>
        <h1>
          Connecting to the model
        </h1>
        Title of steve's favorite: %s
      </body>
    </html>''' % (
        .
        .
        .
    )
    return HttpResponse(output)
```

Listing 4.13 The edited views.py file.

```
from django.http import HttpResponse
from django.contrib.auth.models import User
from favorites.models import *

def main_page(request):
  user = User.objects.get(username='steve')
  title = Favorite.objects.get(user=user).
title
  output = '''
    <html>
      <head>
        <title>
          Connecting to the model
        </title>
      </head>
      <body>
        <h1>
          Connecting to the model
        </h1>
        Title of steve's favorite: %s
      </body>
    </html>''' % (
        title
    )
  return HttpResponse(output)
```

Listing 4.14 The completed views.py file.

2. Add the code to actually access the title of the user's favorite and display it, shown in **Listing 4.14**.

3. Save views.py.

4. Open a command prompt and navigate to the chapter4 directory:

   $ cd django-1.1\django\bin\chapter4

5. Run the development server:

   $ python manage.py runserver

6. Navigate your browser to http://localhost:8000.

   You should see the Web page shown in **Figure 4.5**.

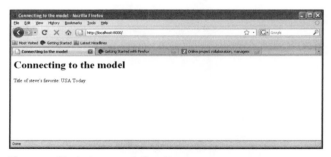

Figure 4.5 Displaying a user's favorite.

Accessing All Favorites for a User

Given a User object, you can find all the favorites of that user by using the expression `user.favorite_set.all()`.

When you get all the favorites of a user, you can loop over them, displaying all their titles like this:

```
from favorites.models import *
def main_page(request):
  user = User.objects.
    get(username='steve')
  favorites = user.favorite_set.all()
  list = ''
  for favorite in favorites:
    list = list + favorite.title + ' <br> '
```

We'll now find the titles of all the favorites of a particular user.

To find all favorites of a particular user:

1. Using a text editor, edit chapter4\favorites\views.py, adding the code shown in **Listing 4.15**.

```
from django.http import HttpResponse
from django.contrib.auth.models import User
from favorites.models import *
def main_page(request):
  user = User.objects.get(username='steve')
  output = '''
  <html>
    <head>
      <title>
        Connecting to the model
      </title>
    </head>
    <body>
      <h1>
        Connecting to the model
      </h1>
      All of steve's favorites: %s
    </body>
  </html>''' % (
    .
    .
    .
  )
  return HttpResponse(output)
```

Listing 4.15 The edited views.py file.

```
from django.http import HttpResponse
from django.contrib.auth.models import User
from favorites.models import *
def main_page(request):
  user = User.objects.get(username='steve')
  favorites = user.favorite_set.all()
  list = ''
  for favorite in favorites:
    list = list + favorite.title + ' <br> '
  output = '''
    <html>
      <head>
        <title>
          Connecting to the model
        </title>
      </head>
      <body>
        <h1>
          Connecting to the model
        </h1>
        All of steve's favorites: %s
      </body>
    </html>''' % (
      list
    )
  return HttpResponse(output)
```

Listing 4.16 The completed views.py file.

2. Add the code to actually access all the user's favorites and display them, shown in **Listing 4.16**.

3. Save views.py.

4. Open a command prompt and navigate to the chapter4 directory:

   `$ cd django-1.1\django\bin\chapter4`

5. Run the development server:

   `$ python manage.py runserver`

6. Navigate your browser to http://localhost:8000.

   You should see the Web page shown in **Figure 4.6**.

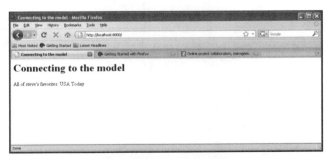

Figure 4.6 Displaying all a user's favorites.

Editing a Favorite

Do you want to edit a field of a particular Favorite object? It's easy. You just access the object you want, edit the fields you want, and save the object in the database:

```
favorite = Favorite.objects.get(id=1)
favorite.title = "Washington Post"
favorite.save()
```

The next time you access the field from the database, it will contain the new data:

```
title = Favorite.objects.get(id=1).title
```

Let's look at this process in action.

To edit a Favorite object:

1. Using a text editor, edit chapter4\
   favorites\views.py, adding the code
   shown in **Listing 4.17**.

```
from django.http import HttpResponse
from django.contrib.auth.models import User
from favorites.models import *

def main_page(request):
    favorite = Favorite.objects.get(id=1)
    favorite.title = "Washington Post"
    favorite.save()
        .
        .
        .
    output = '''
      <html>
        <head>
          <title>
            Connecting to the model
          </title>
        </head>
        <body>
          <h1>
            Connecting to the model
          </h1>
          The edited favorite title: %s
        </body>
      </html>''' % (
        .
        .
        .
    )
    return HttpResponse(output)
```

Listing 4.17 The edited views.py file.

```
from django.http import HttpResponse
from django.contrib.auth.models import User
from favorites.models import *

def main_page(request):
  favorite = Favorite.objects.get(id=1)
  favorite.title = "Washington Post"
  favorite.save()
  title = Favorite.objects.get(id=1).title
  output = '''
    <html>
      <head>
        <title>
          Connecting to the model
        </title>
      </head>
      <body>
        <h1>
          Connecting to the model
        </h1>
        The edited favorite title: %s
      </body>
    </html>''' % (
        title
    )
  return HttpResponse(output)
```

Listing 4.18 The completed views.py file.

2. Add the code to actually access the edited title and display it, shown in **Listing 4.18**.

3. Save views.py.

4. Open a command prompt and navigate to the chapter4 directory:

```
$ cd django-1.1\django\bin\chapter4
```

5. Run the development server:

```
$ python manage.py runserver
```

6. Navigate your browser to http://localhost:8000.

You should see the Web page that appears in **Figure 4.7**.

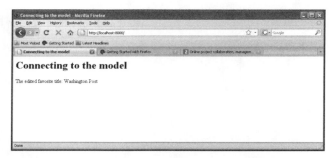

Figure 4.7 Displaying an edited Favorite object.

Creating a New User

Editing fields in a database as we did in the previous topic is fine if the object you want to work with already exists. But what if it doesn't? What if you want to create a new object in the database yourself, from code?

For example, how would you create a new User object? For that, you can use the `create_user` method and then save the new User object, like this:

```
user = User.objects.create_user(
  username = 'nancy',
  password = 'opensesame',
  email = 'nancy@nancy.com'
)
user.save()
```

Here, we'll create a new user and then get the user's email address to confirm that the new user exists.

To create a new user:

1. Using a text editor, edit chapter4\ favorites\views.py, adding the code shown in **Listing 4.19**.

```
from django.http import HttpResponse
from django.contrib.auth.models import User
from favorites.models import *
def main_page(request):
  user = User.objects.create_user(
    username = 'nancy',
    password = 'opensesame',
    email = 'nancy@nancy.com'
  )
  user.save()
        .
        .
        .
  output = '''
    <html>
      <head>
        <title>
          Connecting to the model
        </title>
      </head>
      <body>
        <h1>
          Connecting to the model
        </h1>
        The new user's email: %s
      </body>
    </html>''' % (
    )
  return HttpResponse(output)
```

Listing 4.19 The edited views.py file.

```
from django.http import HttpResponse
from django.contrib.auth.models import User
from favorites.models import *
def main_page(request):
  user = User.objects.create_user(
    username = 'nancy',
    password = 'opensesame',
    email = 'nancy@nancy.com'
  )
  user.save()
  email = User.objects.
    get(username='nancy').email
  output = '''
    <html>
      <head>
        <title>
          Connecting to the model
        </title>
      </head>
      <body>
        <h1>
          Connecting to the model
        </h1>
        The new user's email: %s
      </body>
    </html>''' % (
      email
    )
  return HttpResponse(output)
```

Listing 4.20 The completed views.py file.

2. Add the code to actually access the new user's email address and display it, shown in **Listing 4.20**.

3. Save views.py.

4. Open a command prompt and navigate to the chapter4 directory:

$ `cd django-1.1\django\bin\chapter4`

5. Run the development server:

$ `python manage.py runserver`

6. Navigate your browser to http://localhost:8000.

You should see the Web page shown in **Figure 4.8**.

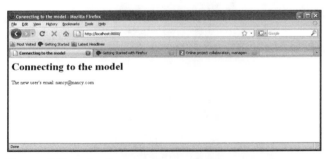

Figure 4.8 Displaying the new user's email address.

CREATING
MULTI-PAGE
WEB APPLICATIONS

5

In the previous chapters, we developed Web applications that had only one page: the main page. In this chapter, we'll start creating multi-page Web applications. In particular, we'll add pages to our application for each user in the database. Each page won't actually exist, though, and just sit around waiting for the user to access it. Instead, the user pages will be created on the fly.

You create pages with code in views.py in a Django application, and for that reason we'll be adding code beyond the main page to our application in this chapter. We'll get Django to help by informing us what page the user is actually accessing, so we'll be able to retrieve the user's data and display it later in this chapter.

Note that we'll also have to build a new template: one for the user pages. In fact, you can build a separate template for every user if you like, but that's not really necessary. Here, we'll build one template for all user pages and fill it with data as appropriate for the individual user.

In coming chapters, we'll let users register themselves on the main page so that they are added as users to the database automatically. We'll also let users log in and log out.

In this chapter, then, we will build a new project, chapter5, and a new application within it, named favorites (we can copy the database from previous chapters, saving us time, since the tables in the database begin with the prefix "favorites_"). Then we'll synchronize the database and create the main view.

After that, we'll add the user pages view to views.py and see how to find out which user is actually accessing his or her page. In particular, we'll catch URLs of the form http://localhost:8000/*username*, where *username* is the name of a user, and in our user view we'll get Django to tell us which username was entered in the URL.

Then we'll retrieve that user's data from the database in the user pages view and pass that data to the user pages template for display.

That's all coming up in this chapter as we graduate from single-page to multi-page Web applications.

Creating the Project and Application

We'll start by creating the chapter5 project and the favorites application. As usual, Django will provide us with the framework for these two components, and we'll do the rest.

To create the Django project and application:

1. To create the Django project, use django-admin.py. Open a command prompt and change to the directory that contains that application:

   ```
   $ cd Django-1.1\django\bin
   ```

   As usual, it is not necessary to run django-admin.py from Django's bin directory. You can run this program from anywhere if you specify the path to it.

2. Run django-admin.py, telling it you want to start a new project named chapter5:

   ```
   $ python django-admin.py
       startproject chapter5
   ```

   The django-admin.py program creates a new directory under the current directory named chapter5.

3. Change to the chapter5 directory:

   ```
   $ cd chapter5
   ```

4. Run the manage.py program to create the new application named favorites:

   ```
   $ python manage.py startapp favorites
   ```

5. Tell Django about your new application, favorites. Open settings.py in the chapter5 project's directory and find the INSTALLED_APPS section, as shown in **Listing 5.1**.

```
INSTALLED_APPS = (
    'django.contrib.auth',
    'django.contrib.contenttypes',
    'django.contrib.sessions',
    'django.contrib.sites',
)
```

Listing 5.1 The settings.py file.

```
INSTALLED_APPS = (
    'django.contrib.auth',
    'django.contrib.contenttypes',
    'django.contrib.sessions',
    'django.contrib.sites',
    'chapter5.favorites',)
```

Listing 5.2 The edited settings.py file.

6. Add a line to tell Django about the chapter5.favorites application, as shown in **Listing 5.2**.

7. Save the file.

Now we have a new project, chapter5, and a new application, favorites. The next step is to copy the database file, favoritesdb, that we previously loaded with data.

Installing the Database

Django applications usually rely on their databases, and our application in this chapter will be no exception. To save the time, we'll copy the database from a previous chapter.

The copy process involves these steps:

◆ Copy favoritesdb.

◆ Copy models.py.

◆ Edit settings.py to make the database favoritesdb.

◆ Synchronize the database.

To transfer the database:

1. Copy the database, favoritesdb, from the chapter3 or chapter4 folder to the chapter5 folder.

2. Copy models.py from chapter3\favorites or chapter4\favorites to chapter5\favorites. (If your operating system asks whether you want to replace the existing models.py file, answer Yes.)

✔ Tip

■ You can copy the database, favoritesdb, from either Chapter 3 or Chapter 4— they're equivalent for this chapter.

```
INSTALLED_APPS = (
    'django.contrib.auth',
    'django.contrib.contenttypes',
    'django.contrib.sessions',
    'django.contrib.sites',
    'chapter5.favorites',)
```

Listing 5.3 The settings.py file.

```
DATABASE_ENGINE = 'sqlite3'          #
    'postgresql_psycopg2',
    'postgresql', 'mysql', 'sqlite3'
    or 'oracle'.
DATABASE_NAME = 'favoritesdb'        #
    Or path
    to database file if using
    sqlite3.
DATABASE_USER = ''            # Not used
    with sqlite3.
DATABASE_PASSWORD = ''        # Not used
    with sqlite3.
```

Listing 5.4 The edited settings.py file.

3. Using a text-editing program, open chapter5\settings.py and find the database section, shown in **Listing 5.3**.

4. Enter **'sqlite3'** for the DATABASE_ ENGINE setting and **favoritesdb** for the DATABASE_NAME setting (**Listing 5.4**).

5. Save the file.

6. Open a command prompt, and in the chapter5 directory, enter this command to set up the database system:

   `$ python manage.py syncdb`

   You will not be prompted to create a superuser account, since that account already exists in the chapter3 favoritesdb database.

The database is set up, having been transferred from the chapter3 or chapter4 project.

Creating the Main View

The next step in getting our favorites application running is to create the main view. That's the default page that the application will display if you haven't specified that you want to see a particular user's page.

Creating the main view involves two steps: writing views.py and then editing urls.py to tell Django about the view we've set up.

To create the main view:

1. Using a text editor, edit chapter5\favorites\views.py to add a new view named main_page, replacing the current version of views.py with the code shown in **Listing 5.5**.

✔ Tip

■ In Python, code indentation counts, so be sure to indent properly.

This version of views.py simply displays a placeholder Web page.

```
from django.http import HttpResponse

def main_page(request):
  output = '''
    <html>
      <head>
        <title>
          Creating multi-page
            applications
        </title>
      </head>
      <body>
        <h1>
          Creating multi-page
            applications
        </h1>
        Enter
          http://localhost:8000/username
          to see a user's page.
      </body>
    </html>'''
  return HttpResponse(output)
```

Listing 5.5 The edited views.py file.

```
from django.conf.urls.defaults import *
from favorites.views import *

# Uncomment the next two lines to enable
    the admin:
# from django.contrib import admin
# admin.autodiscover()

urlpatterns = patterns('',
  (r'^$', main_page),
)
```

Listing 5.6 The edited urls.py file.

2. Save views.py.

3. Edit chapter5\urls.py to add the main_ page view to the application, making the additions shown in **Listing 5.6**.

4. Save urls.py.

5. Open a command prompt and navigate to the chapter5 directory:

   ```
   $ cd django-1.1\django\bin\chapter5
   ```

6. Run the development server:

   ```
   $ python manage.py runserver
   ```

7. Navigate your browser to http:// localhost:8000.

   You should see the Web page shown in **Figure 5.1**.

Figure 5.1 Starting our favorites application.

Setting Up the User URLs

We've already set up the main page URL in urls.py, connecting it to the `main_page()` function like this:

```
urlpatterns = patterns('',
  (r'^$', main_page),
```

Now we need to connect the user pages to URLs as well. Our goal is to allow the user to enter a URL like http://localhost:80000/steve and have Steve's user page appear.

You can do that with a regular expression as shown here, where \w stands for a word character such as a letter or number, and \w+ means one or more word characters:

```
urlpatterns = patterns('',
  (r'^$', main_page),
  (r'^(\w+)/$', user_page),
```

This line connects user URLs to a function named `user_page()`, which we'll add to views.py in the next task.

Note the parentheses around \w+; they make Django capture the username entered and pass it to us in the `user_page()` function, as you'll see in the next chapter.

Now let's set up the URLs for the user pages.

To set up the user URLs:

1. Using a text editor, edit chapter5\favorites\urls.py (**Listing 5.7**).

2. Add the code to connect user pages to the `user_page()` function (**Listing 5.8**).

3. Save urls.py.

This task connects user pages, entered as http://localhost:8000/username, to the view function `user_page()`. We'll write that function in the next task.

```
from django.conf.urls.defaults import *
from favorites.views import *


# Uncomment the next two lines to enable
    the admin:
# from django.contrib import admin
# admin.autodiscover()
```

Listing 5.7 The current urls.py file.

```
from django.conf.urls.defaults import *
from favorites.views import *

# Uncomment the next two lines to enable
    the admin:
# from django.contrib import admin
# admin.autodiscover()

urlpatterns = patterns('',
  (r'^$', main_page),
  (r'^(\w+)/$', user_page),
)
```

Listing 5.8 The completed urls.py file.

```
from django.http import HttpResponse

def main_page(request):
  output = '''
    <html>
      <head>
        <title>
          Creating multi-page
        applications
        </title>
      </head>
      <body>
        <h1>
          Creating multi-page
        applications
        </h1>
          Enter http://localhost:8000/username
to see a user's page.
      </body>
    </html>'''
  return HttpResponse(output)


def user_page(request, username):
  output = '''
    <html>
      <head>
        <title>
          User pages
        </title>
      </head>
      <body>
        <h1>
          User pages
        </h1>
        You have reached %s's page.
      </body>
    </html>''' % (
      username
    )
  return HttpResponse(output)
```

Listing 5.9 The completed views.py file.

Creating the User Views

At this point, views.py contains only a function named `main_page()`:

```
from django.http import HttpResponse

def main_page(request):
  output = '''
    <html>
      <head>
        <title>
          .
          .
          .
```

We want to add support for our new user pages in a function called `user_page()`:

```
def user_page(request, username):
  output = '''
    <html>
      <head>
          .
          .
          .
```

Note in particular that we're passed the username the user entered as part of the URL (because we enclosed that part of the URL in parentheses in urls.py). In this task, we'll verify that we received the username by displaying it in the user's page.

To create the user views:

1. Using a text editor, edit chapter5\favorites\views.py.

2. Add the `user_page()` function to display the name of the user in a user page (**Listing 5.9**).

continues on next page

3. Save views.py.

4. Open a command prompt and navigate to the chapter5 directory:

```
$ cd django-1.1\django\bin\chapter5
```

5. Run the development server:

```
$ python manage.py runserver
```

6. Navigate your browser to http://localhost:8000/*username*, where *username* is any name.

You should see the Web page shown in **Figure 5.2**. Notice that it even displays the user's name in the page.

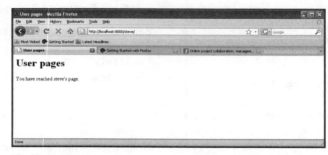

Figure 5.2 A user's page.

```
TEMPLATE_DIRS = (
    # Put strings here, like
        "/home/html/django_templates" or
        "C:/www/django/templates".
    # Always use forward slashes, even on
        Windows.
    # Don't forget to use absolute paths,
        not relative paths.
    )
```

Listing 5.10 The original settings.py file.

```
TEMPLATE_DIRS = (
    # Put strings here, like
        "/home/html/django_templates" or
        "C:/www/django/templates".
    # Always use forward slashes, even on
        Windows.
    # Don't forget to use absolute paths,
        not relative paths.
    "C:/django/Django-
    1.1/django/bin/chapter5/templates
    "
```

Listing 5.11 The completed settings.py file.

Setting Up the Template

So far, we've displayed a user page directly from the view, but that's the procedure in only the most basic Django applications. In full Django applications, you let the view call a template to render the final Web page.

To set up templates in our applications, we'll create a templates directory and then create the template itself: user_page.html. We'll then have to connect the view to the template, and we'll do that in the next few tasks.

We'll begin setting up the application to work with templates by creating a templates directory.

To set up the template:

1. Open a command prompt and change to the chapter5 directory:

   ```
   $ cd django-1.1\django\bin\chapter5
   ```

2. Create a new directory named templates:

   ```
   $ md templates
   ```

   Now we need to tell Django about the new templates directory.

3. In a text editor, open chapter5\settings.py and find the TEMPLATE_DIRS section (**Listing 5.10**).

4. Add the code to add the new templates directory to the application by specifying that directory's full path (**Listing 5.11**).

5. Save settings.py.

The templates directory for our application is set up. Next, we'll set up the actual template for the user pages: user_page.html.

Creating the User Template

In this task, we'll create a basic user template for our application. The task involves creating the HTML file that will be used as a template—user_page.html—and editing its contents. In the next task, we'll set up the view to call this template so we can see it in a Web browser.

To create the user template:

1. Using a text editor, create the document user_page.html in the templates directory, adding the contents shown in **Listing 5.12**.

2. Add the <head> section to the template (**Listing 5.13**).

3. Add the <body> section of the user template (**Listing 5.14**). Here, for the body of the template, we'll include just a message, "Welcome to the user pages."

4. Save user_page.html.

We have set up the templates directory and connected it to the application and created the template itself. The final step in installing the template and getting it working is to make the view in our application load and call the template, and that's coming up in the next task.

```
<html>
            .
            .
            .
</html>
```

Listing 5.12 Starting user_page.html.

```
<html>
  <head>
    <title>User pages</title>
  </head>
        .
        .
        .
</html>
```

Listing 5.13 Adding the <head> section.

```
<html>
  <head>
    <title>User pages</title>
  </head>
  <body>
    <h1>User pages</h1>
    Welcome to the user pages.
  </body>
</html>
```

Listing 5.14 The completed template.

```
from django.http import HttpResponse

def main_page(request):
  output = '''
    <html>
      <head>
        <title>
          Creating multi-page  applications
        </title>
      </head>
      <body>
        <h1>
          Creating multi-page  applications
        </h1>
        Enter  http://localhost:8000/
            username to
            see a user's page.
      </body>
    </html>'''
  return HttpResponse(output)

def user_page(request, username):
  output = '''
    <html>
      <head>
        <title>
          User pages
        </title>
      </head>
      <body>
        <h1>
          User pages
        </h1>
        You have reached %s's page.
      </body>
    </html>''' % (
      username
    )
  return HttpResponse(output)
```

Listing 5.15 The original views.py file.

Making the View Call the Template

To make the template active in an application, you have to load it in the view and ask it to render the output you want to send to the browser. Accordingly, we'll edit the view in our application to load the template and connect its output to the browser.

To make the view call the template:

1. Using a text editor, open chapter5\favorites\views.py (**Listing 5.15**).

continues on next page

2. Change the `user_page()` function to load the template and send its output to the browser (**Listing 5.16**).

   Note that the template's render method requires a Context object to be passed to it, so we will pass it an empty object here (since the template as written doesn't use a Context object yet).

3. Save views.py.

4. Open a command prompt and navigate to the chapter5 directory:

   `$ cd django-1.1\django\bin\chapter5`

5. Run the development server:

   `$ python manage.py runserver`

6. Navigate your browser to http://localhost:8000/*username*, where *username* is any name.

   You should see the Web page shown in **Figure 5.3**.

```python
from django.http import HttpResponse
from django.template import Context
from django.template.loader import
    get_template
        .
        .
        .
def user_page(request, username):
    template =  get_template('user_page.html')

    variables = Context({
    })
    output = template.render(variables)
    return HttpResponse(output)
```

Listing 5.16 The completed views.py file.

Figure 5.3 The output from a basic template.

```
from django.http import HttpResponse
from django.template import Context
from django.template.loader import get_
template

def main_page(request):
  output = '''
    <html>
      <head>
        <title>
          Creating multi-page  applications
        </title>
      </head>
      <body>
        <h1>
          Creating multi-page  applications
        </h1>
        Enter  http://localhost:8000/
            username to
            see a user's page.
      </body>
    </html>'''
  return HttpResponse(output)

def user_page(request, username):
  template =  get_template('user_page.html')
  variables = Context({
   'username': username
  })
  output = template.render(variables)
  return HttpResponse(output)
```

Listing 5.17 The edited views.py file.

Passing User Data to the Template

In this task, we'll connect the view to the template as we pass the user's name (as entered in the URL) to the template for display.

We'll have to modify both the view and the template. The view will now have to load the data to be passed to the Context object sent to the template, and the template will have to retrieve the data from that object.

To pass user data to the template:

1. Using a text editor, edit chapter5\favorites\views.py, adding the code shown in **Listing 5.17**.

   This code adds to the template the username passed to us in the user_page() function.

2. Save views.py.

continues on next page

3. Using a text editor, retrieve the data passed to the template and display the user's name in the body of the Web page (**Listing 5.18**).

4. Save user_page.py.

5. Open a command prompt and navigate to the chapter5 directory:

   ```
   $ cd django-1.1\django\bin\chapter5
   ```

6. Run the development server:

   ```
   $ python manage.py runserver
   ```

7. Navigate your browser to http://localhost:8000/*username*, where *username* is any name.

   You should see the Web page shown in **Figure 5.4**.

```
from django.http import HttpResponse

<html>
  <head>
    <title>User pages</title>
  </head>
  <body>
    <h1>User pages</h1>
    Welcome to {{ username }}'s page.
  </body>
</html>
```

Listing 5.18 The edited user_page.html file.

Figure 5.4 Displaying the user's name.

```
from django.http import HttpResponse, Http404
from django.contrib.auth.models import User
from django.template import Context
from django.template.loader import
    get_template

def main_page(request):
    .
    .
    .
  return HttpResponse(output)

def user_page(request, username):
  user =
    User.objects.get(username=username)

  favorites = user.favorite_set.all()

  template =  get_template('user_page.html')
  variables = Context({
    'username': username,
    'favorites': favorites
  })

  output = template.render(variables)
  return HttpResponse(output)
```

Listing 5.19 The edited views.py file.

```
<html>
  <head>
    <title>User pages</title>
  </head>
  <body>
    <h1>User pages</h1>
    Here are {{ username }}'s favorites:
        {% for favorite in favorites %}
          <br>
          <a href="{{
             favorite.hyperlink.url }}">
           {{ favorite.title }}</a>
        {% endfor %}
  </body>
</html>
```

Listing 5.20 The completed user_page.html file.

Displaying a User's Favorites

The next step is to dig some data out of the database and pass it to the template to be displayed. In this case, we'll display all the user's favorites in the browser—that is, to see all a user's favorites, all you'll have to do is go to the user's Web page, and the favorites, as stored in the database, will all be shown.

In this task, we'll edit the view so it retrieves data from the model and passes that data to the template. We'll also change the template to loop over the passed data to display the user's name and favorites.

To display a user's favorites:

1. Using a text editor, edit chapter5\
favorites\views.py, adding the code
shown in **Listing 5.19**.

   This code adds a set of all the user's
   favorites to the Context object passed
   to the template.

2. Save views.py.

3. Edit user_page.html, adding the code
shown in **Listing 5.20**.

✔ Tip

■ Note that you can execute Python code
in the template if you surround that code
with {% and %}—a very important feature
of Django.

continues on next page

4. Save user_page.html.

5. Open a command prompt and navigate to the chapter5 directory:

   ```
   $ cd django-1.1\django\bin\chapter5
   ```

6. Run the development server:

   ```
   $ python manage.py runserver
   ```

7. Navigate your browser to http://localhost:8000/*username*, where *username* is the name of a user in your database (such as the superuser).

   You should see the Web page shown in **Figure 5.5**. This user has only one favorite stored in the database, and that's what you see in the figure.

Figure 5.5 Displaying a user's favorites.

STYLING DJANGO WEB PAGES

Let's say you have this perfectly ordinary style sheet style.css:

```
body {
  color: red;
}
h1 {
  color: blue;
}
p {
  color: green;
}
```

This style sheet styles <body> text in Web pages red, <h1> headers blue, and <p> elements green (perhaps not the most pleasing color scheme). How do you apply this style sheet to a Django Web page with <body> text, <h1> headers, and <p> elements?

Many Web servers will serve your style sheet in addition to your Django application, but some (like the development server we've been using) will not, because they leave the delivery of Django content up to Django. To make sure that your style sheets are served to your Django application no matter what Django-enabled server you're using (including the development server), use the techniques in this chapter.

To get Django to handle static style sheets by default and make them available to your Web applications, you use a Django class, written in Python, to load static pages for you. Setting up the static page loader is pretty simple, but you have to know what you're doing.

The actual work is done in urls.py. After you create a new directory for your style sheets, you connect URLs accessing that directory to the static page loader in urls.py. Then when one of your pages (using a <link> element) references a style sheet, that style sheet will be found and applied no matter what Django-enabled server you're using.

We'll create a new application in this chapter—the users application—to see how to apply style sheets in Django applications.

Creating the users Application

We'll start by creating the chapter6 project and the users application. As usual, Django will provide the framework for these two components, and we'll do the rest.

To create the Django project and application:

1. Open a command prompt window and change to the directory that contains that application:

   ```
   $ cd Django-1.1\django\bin
   ```

   (If you prefer, you can run this program from elsewhere by specifying the path to it.)

2. Run django-admin.py, telling it you want to start a new project named chapter6.

   ```
   $ python django-admin.py
       startproject chapter6
   ```

   The django-admin.py program creates a new directory under the current directory named chapter6.

3. Change to the chapter6 directory:

   ```
   $ cd chapter6
   ```

4. Run the manage.py program to create the new application named users:

   ```
   $ python manage.py startapp users
   ```

5. You have to tell Django about your new application, users, so open settings.py in the chapter6 project's directory and find the INSTALLED_APPS section, shown in **Listing 6.1**.

6. Add a line to tell Django about the chapter6.users application, as shown in **Listing 6.2**.

7. Save the file.

Now we have a new project, chapter6, and a new application, users.

```
INSTALLED_APPS = (
    'django.contrib.auth',
    'django.contrib.contenttypes',
    'django.contrib.sessions',
    'django.contrib.sites',
)
```

Listing 6.1 The settings.py file.

```
INSTALLED_APPS = (
    'django.contrib.auth',
    'django.contrib.contenttypes',
    'django.contrib.sessions',
    'django.contrib.sites',
    'chapter6.users',)
```

Listing 6.2 The edited settings.py file.

```
DATABASE_ENGINE = 'sqlite3'        #
    'postgresql_psycopg2',
    'postgresql', 'mysql', 'sqlite3'
    or 'oracle'.
DATABASE_NAME = 'usersdb'          #
    Or path
    to database file if using
    sqlite3.
```

Listing 6.3 The edited settings.py file.

```
from django.db import models
from django.contrib.auth.models import User
```

Listing 6.4 The edited models.py file.

Creating the Database

The users application will store information about various users and display it in the main view. To make that happen, we'll set up a model and install a few users in it.

To create the database:

1. Edit chapter6\settings.py and enter **'sqlite3'** for the DATABASE_ENGINE setting and **usersdb** for the DATABASE_NAME setting (**Listing 6.3**).

2. Save settings.py.

3. Edit chapter6\users\models.py by adding the text shown in **Listing 6.4** to add the Django User model to the application.

4. Save models.py.

5. Open a command prompt window, and in the chapter6 directory enter this command to set up the database system:

   ```
   $ python manage.py syncdb
   ```

   continues on next page

6. When prompted to create a superuser for the database, enter this data:

You just installed Django's auth system, which means you don't have any superusers defined.

Would you like to create one now? (yes/no):

Enter **yes**.

Username:

Enter a name.

E-mail address:

Enter an email address.

Password:

Enter a password.

Password (again):

Enter the password again.

7. Create two more users. Start the shell and enter something like this (entering your own user information):

```
$ python manage.py shell
>>> from django.contrib.auth.models
import User
>>> User.objects.create_user(
... username='nancy',
... email='nancy@nancy.com',
... password='opensesame'
... )
>>> User.objects.create_user(
... username='tamsen',
... email='tamsen@tamsen.com',
... password='opensesame'
... )
>>>exit()
```

Good—the database is set up.

```
from django.http import HttpResponse
from django.contrib.auth.models import User
from django.template import Context
from django.template.loader import
    get_template


def main_page(request):
  template = get_template('main_page.html')
        .
        .
        .

  return HttpResponse(output)
```

Listing 6.5 The edited views.py file.

```
from django.http import HttpResponse
from django.contrib.auth.models import User
from django.template import Context
from django.template.loader import
    get_template


def main_page(request):
  template = get_template('main_page.html')
  username1 = User.objects.get(id=1).username
  username2 = User.objects.get(id=2).username
  username3 = User.objects.get(id=3).username
  variables = Context({
    'username1': username1,
    'username2': username2,
    'username3': username3
  })
  output = template.render(variables)
  return HttpResponse(output)
```

Listing 6.6 The completed views.py file.

Creating the View

Next we'll create the users application view, which will grab the user data from the database and send it to the template.

To create the view:

1. Using a text editor, edit chapter6\users\ views.py to add a new view named main_page, replacing the current version of views.py with the code in **Listing 6.5**.

2. Add to the view the code to fetch the user data and pass the users' names to the template, main_page.html (**Listing 6.6**).

3. Save views.py.

✔ Tip

■ In Python, code indentation counts, so be sure to indent properly.

Creating the Template

The template is the part of the application responsible for rendering the Web page—and the template is the part of the application to which we want to apply our style sheets.

We'll start by creating the template and then making sure that our users application is working before creating our style sheet and applying it to the template.

To create the template:

1. Open a command prompt window and change to the chapter6 directory:

   `$ cd \django-1.1\django\bin\chapter6`

2. Create a new directory to hold our templates, naming the directory templates:

   `$ md templates`

3. Using a text editor, create the template chapter6\templates\main_page.html and add the contents shown in **Listing 6.7**.

   This template is designed to display the names of the three users in the database in <p> elements.

4. Save main_page.html.

5. Add the new templates directory to the TEMPLATE_DIRS section of settings.py, as shown in **Listing 6.8**.

```
<html>
  <head>
    <title>The users application</title>
  </head>
  <body>
    <h1>The users application</h1>
    Here are the users:
    <p>{{ username1 }} </p>
    <p>{{ username2 }} </p>
    <p>{{ username3 }} </p>
  </body>
</html>
```

Listing 6.7 The main_page.html file.

```
TEMPLATE_DIRS = (
"C:/django/Django-1.1/django/bin/chapter6/
    templates"
)
```

Listing 6.8 The settings.py file.

```
from django.conf.urls.defaults import *
from users.views import *

# Uncomment the next two lines to enable
    the admin:
# from django.contrib import admin
# admin.autodiscover()

urlpatterns = patterns('',
  (r'^$', main_page)
)
```

Listing 6.9 The completed urls.py file.

6. Edit chapter6\urls.py to connect the view to the application (**Listing 6.9**).

7. Save urls.py.
   Now we'll test the application so far.

8. In the command prompt window, navigate to the chapter6 directory:
   `$ cd django-1.1\django\bin\chapter6`

9. Run the development server:
   `$ python manage.py runserver`

10. Navigate your browser to http://localhost:8000.
    You should see the Web page shown in **Figure 6.1**.

Figure 6.1 shows the users application without any formatting—the users' names just appear as plain text. We'll work on creating and applying a style sheet next.

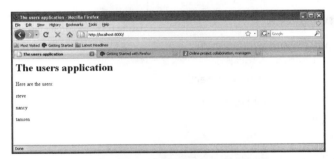

Figure 6.1 Starting our users application.

Creating the Style Sheet

The style sheets you can use with Django applications are the standard style sheets that all browsers understand. For example, you can create such a style sheet from style rules, which connect an element type (such as <body> or <h1>) with a style property (such as color) and a setting (such as red):

```
element {
  property: setting;
}

element {
  property: setting;
}

element {
  property: setting;
}
```

We'll create a standard style sheet in this task and then apply it to our Django template.

To create the style sheet:

1. Open a command prompt window and change to the chapter6 directory:

   `$ cd \django-1.1\django\bin\chapter6`

2. Create a new directory to hold our style sheet, named stylesheets:

   `$ md stylesheets`

3. Using a text editor, create chapter6\stylesheets\style.css.

4. Add the style rule to display <body> text in 12-point font, as shown in **Listing 6.10**.

5. Add style rules for <h1> headers and <p> elements to the style sheet (**Listing 6.11**).

6. Save style.css.

That completes the style sheet, style.css, and installs it in the stylesheets directory. Now we need to tell Django to serve this style sheet when needed, and that's coming up in the next task.

```
body {
  font-size: 12pt;
}
         .
         .
         .
```

Listing 6.10 The style.css file.

```
body {
  font-size: 12pt;
}

h1 {
  color: red;
}


p {
  font-size: 20pt;
}
```

Listing 6.11 The completed style.css file.

```
import os.path
from django.conf.urls.defaults import *
from users.views import *

# Uncomment the next two lines to enable
    the admin:
# from django.contrib import admin
# admin.autodiscover()

stylesheets = os.path.join(os.path.
    dirname(__file__), 'stylesheets')

urlpatterns = patterns('',
  (r'^$', main_page),
        .
        .
```

Listing 6.12 The urls.py file.

```
import os.path
from django.conf.urls.defaults import *
from users.views import *

# Uncomment the next two lines to enable
    the admin:
# from django.contrib import admin
# admin.autodiscover()

stylesheets = os.path.join(os.path.
    dirname(__file__), 'stylesheets')

urlpatterns = patterns('',
  (r'^$', main_page),
  (r'^stylesheets/(?P<path>.*)$',
    'django.views.static.serve',
    { 'document_root': stylesheets }),
```

Listing 6.13 The completed urls.py file.

Making Django Serve the Style Sheet

To make the style sheet available to our template, we have to make sure it's served to the browser. While some Django-enabled servers will do that, some won't, so we'll make sure that Django itself handles the job in this task.

We've put our style sheet in the stylesheets directory, and now we have to make sure that Django serves any document from that directory or its subdirectory to the browser, even if that document, like a style sheet, is static.

You can serve static documents with the Django class `django.views.static.serve`.

To make Django serve the style sheet:

1. In a text editor, open chapter6\urls.py and make the changes shown in **Listing 6.12**, storing the absolute path of the stylesheets directory in a variable named stylesheets.

2. Connect the stylesheets directory to URLs that contain the style sheets in the path (**Listing 6.13**).

3. Save urls.py.

We've set up Django to serve the style sheet. Next, we have to connect the style sheet to the template.

Connecting the Style Sheet to the Template

To connect the style sheet to the template, we have to add HTML to the template, as with any style sheet. In particular, we need to add a `<link>` element like this to the template:

```
<link rel="stylesheet"
  href="/stylesheets/style.css"
  type="text/css" />
```

Here, we're linking to style.css in the stylesheets directory—and we've set up urls.py so that Django will serve style.css from the stylesheets directory, even though it's a static document.

To connect the style sheet to the template:

1. With a text editor, add the `<link>` element shown in **Listing 6.14** to chapter6\templates\main_page.html to indicate that you want to style the current document with the style.css document from the stylesheets directory.

2. Save main_page.html.

```
<html>
  <head>
    <title>The users application</title>
    <link rel="stylesheet"
      href="/stylesheets/style.css"
      type="text/css" />
  </head>
  <body>
    <h1>The users application</h1>
    Here are the users:
    <p>{{ username1 }} </p>
    <p>{{ username2 }} </p>
    <p>{{ username3 }} </p>
  </body>
</html>
```

Listing 6.14 The completed main_page.html file.

3. Open a command prompt window and navigate to the chapter6 directory:

```
$ cd django-1.1\django\bin\chapter6
```

4. Run the development server:

```
$ python manage.py runserver
```

5. Navigate your browser to http://localhost:8000.

You should see the styled Web page shown in **Figure 6.2**.

Great—you can see the styles in style.css applied to the template in Figure 6.2. Now you're applying styles to Django applications.

Figure 6.2 Our styled Web page.

Making Style Changes to the Template

Now that you've connected a style sheet to the template, you can easily make changes to that style sheet. For example, in this task, we'll color the background of the page that the template renders, giving the page a pink background in the browser.

To change the styling of the template:

1. Using a text editor, open chapter6\ stylesheets\style.css (**Listing 6.15**).

2. Add the line shown in **Listing 6.16** to style the page's background pink.

3. Save style.css.

4. Open a command prompt window and change to the chapter6 directory:

   `$ cd django-1.1\django\bin\chapter6`

5. Run the development server (if you were already running the server, you have to restart it):

   `$ python manage.py runserver`

6. Navigate your browser to http:// localhost:8000/*username*, where *username* is any name.

   You should see the Web page shown in **Figure 6.3**.

```
body {
    font-size: 12pt;
}

h1 {
    color: red;
}


p {
    font-size: 20pt;
}
```

Listing 6.15 The current style.css file.

```
body {
    font-size: 12pt;
    background-color: pink;
}

h1 {
    color: red;
}


p {
    font-size: 20pt;
}
```

Listing 6.16 The edited style.css file.

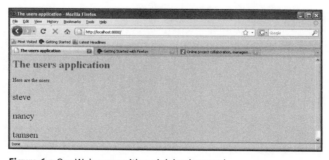

Figure 6.3 Our Web page with a pink background.

```
<html>
  <head>
    <title>The users application</title>
    <link rel="stylesheet" href="/stylesheets/
      style.css" type="text/css" />
  </head>
  <body>
    <h1>The users application</h1>
    Here are the users:
    <p>{{ username1 }} </p>
    <p id="big">{{ username2 }} </p>
    <p>{{ username3 }} </p>
  </body>
</html>
```

Listing 6.17 The edited main_page.html file.

```
from django.http import HttpResponse
body {
  font-size: 12pt;
}


h1 {
  color: red;
}


p {
  font-size: 20pt;
}

#big {
  font-size: 32pt;
}
```

Listing 6.18 The edited style.css file.

Styling by ID

You can also style individual elements in Django pages if you give those elements a particular ID and specify the style you want using that ID.

Here's an example that styles one particular <p> element in a Django Web page so that it displays text in a very large font.

To style Django pages by ID:

1. Using a text editor, edit chapter6\ templates\main_page.html, adding an ID value to the second <p> element as shown in **Listing 6.17**.

2. Save main_page.html.

3. Using a text editor, edit chapter6\ stylesheets\style.css, adding the styling for elements with the ID "big" to make them appear in a larger font (**Listing 6.18**).

4. Save style.css.

continues on next page

5. Open a command prompt window and change to the chapter6 directory:

```
$ cd django-1.1\django\bin\chapter6
```

6. Run the development server:

```
$ python manage.py runserver
```

7. Navigate your browser to http://localhost:8000/*username*, where *username* is any name.

You should see the Web page shown in **Figure 6.4**.

As you can see, you can style any item in a Django page simply by giving the enclosing element an ID and styling by that ID in your style sheet.

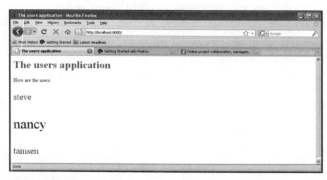

Figure 6.4 Displaying the user's name in a larger font.

INHERITING TEMPLATES

As your applications grow larger, planning them becomes more important. For instance, you may have a Web application of a hundred pages and want to preserve a uniform look and feel across all those pages.

Template inheritance to the rescue! Django lets one template inherit from another, enabling you to easily create a consistent look for your pages—great for company Web sites or any Web site with more than just a few pages. For example, you may want to present a navigation bar at the bottom of all your Web pages and also a copyright notice. You may want to display a menu at the top of all pages and some company information, too. You can do all that easily with template inheritance.

To use template inheritance, you create a base template that has all the common elements you want in all your templates. For example, the base template may contain a navigation bar and copyright notice. Then when you create templates that inherit the base template, they can display the same navigation bar and copyright information. In fact, display of such inherited features becomes automatic; all the templates in your application can automatically inherit the base template and so display all the common features you want with just a few keystrokes.

In addition to helping you maintain a common appearance and a set of common features at a Web site, template inheritance enables you to much more easily maintain a large site. If you need to make a change to your navigation bar, for example, you need to make that change in only one place. You don't need to hunt down all pages that display a navigation bar and make the change in each one; you just change the navigation bar in the base template and you're set.

continues on next page

Employing template inheritance to maintain a site is good practice, even for smaller sites. Even if your site has only a few pages, if they have common features, you should consider template inheritance. You'll be surprised how much time you can save.

In this chapter, we'll extend the users application developed in the previous chapter by adding a template for the main view and a template for the user pages. To see how template inheritance works, we'll then create a base template and let the main template and the user template inherit that base template, letting the base template handle the features common to all templates.

```
INSTALLED_APPS = (
    'django.contrib.auth',
    'django.contrib.contenttypes',
    'django.contrib.sessions',
    'django.contrib.sites',
)
```

Listing 7.1 The settings.py file.

```
INSTALLED_APPS = (
    'django.contrib.auth',
    'django.contrib.contenttypes',
    'django.contrib.sessions',
    'django.contrib.sites',
    'chapter7.users',)
```

Listing 7.2 The edited settings.py file.

Creating the Project and Application

To see how template inheritance works, we'll first create the project, chapter7, and the application, users, in that project.

To create the chapter7 project and application:

1. To create the Django project, use django-admin.py; open a command prompt and change to the directory that contains that application:

   `$ cd Django-1.1\django\bin`

2. Run django-admin.py, telling it you want to start a new project named chapter7:

   `$ python django-admin.py startproject chapter7`

   The django-admin.py program creates a new directory named chapter7 under the current directory.

3. Change to the chapter7 directory:

   `$ cd chapter7`

4. Run the manage.py program to create the new application named users:

   `$ python manage.py startapp users`

5. Tell Django about your new application, users; open settings.py in the chapter7 project's directory and find the INSTALLED_APPS section (**Listing 7.1**).

6. Add a line to tell Django about the chapter7.users application as shown in **Listing 7.2**.

7. Save the file.

Now we have a new project, chapter7, and a new application, users. The next step is to transfer the database file, usersdb, we created so carefully in the previous chapter.

Transferring the Database

We created a database with users in it in Chapter 6. We'll copy that database, usersdb, for use in the chapter7 project.

The copying process involves these steps:

◆ Copy usersdb.

◆ Copy models.py.

◆ Edit settings.py to create the usersdb database.

◆ Synchronize the database.

To transfer the database:

1. Copy the usersdb database from the chapter6 folder to the chapter7 folder. The usersdb database contains the tables and data that we'll use in this chapter.

2. Copy models.py from chapter6\users to chapter7\users. (If your operating system asks whether you want to replace the existing models.py file, answer Yes.)

The models.py file contains the definitions of the models you want to use. Unless you copy the version of models.py created in Chapter 6 that defines the models, you'll lose the models in the database when you synchronize the database.

3. Using a text-editing program, open chapter7\settings.py and find the database section, shown in **Listing 7.3**.

```
DATABASE_ENGINE = ''          #
    'postgresql_psycopg2',
    'postgresql', 'mysql', 'sqlite3'
    or 'oracle'.
DATABASE_NAME = ''            # Or path
    to database file if using
    sqlite3.
DATABASE_USER = ''            # Not used
    with sqlite3.
DATABASE_PASSWORD = ''        # Not used
    with sqlite3.
```

Listing 7.3 The settings.py file.

```
DATABASE_ENGINE = 'sqlite3'           #
    'postgresql_psycopg2',
    'postgresql', 'mysql', 'sqlite3'
    or 'oracle'.
DATABASE_NAME = 'usersdb'             #
    Or path  to database file if using
    sqlite3.
DATABASE_USER = ''           # Not used
    with sqlite3.
DATABASE_PASSWORD = ''       # Not used
    with sqlite3.
```

Listing 7.4 The edited settings.py file.

4. Enter **'sqlite3'** for the DATABASE_ENGINE setting and **usersdb** for the DATABASE_ NAME setting (**Listing 7.4**).

5. Save the file.

6. Open a command prompt, and in the chapter7 directory, enter this command to set up the database system:

   $ python manage.py syncdb

   You will not be prompted to create a superuser account, since that account already exists in the chapter6 usersdb database.

The database is set up, having been transferred from the chapter6 project.

Creating the Main View

Next we'll create the users application main view, which will greet people new to the application.

To create the main view:

1. Using a text editor, edit chapter7\ users\views.py to add a new view named main_page, replacing the current version of views.py with the code shown in **Listing 7.5**.

2. Add the code to pass an empty Context object to the template (**Listing 7.6**).

```
from django.contrib.auth.models import User
from django. from django.http import
    HttpResponse
template import Context
from django.template.loader import
    get_template


def main_page(request):
  template = get_template('main_page.html')
        .
        .
        .

    return HttpResponse(output)
```

Listing 7.5 The edited views.py file.

```
from django.http import HttpResponse
from django.contrib.auth.models import User
from django.template import Context
from django.template.loader import
    get_template

def main_page(request):
  template = get_template('main_page.html')
  variables = Context({
})
  output = template.render(variables)
  return HttpResponse(output)
```

Listing 7.6 The completed views.py file.

```
from django.conf.urls.defaults import *
from users.views import *

# Uncomment the next two lines to enable
    the admin:
# from django.contrib import admin
# admin.autodiscover()

urlpatterns = patterns('',
  (r'^$', main_page),
)
```

Listing 7.7 The urls.py file.

3. Save views.py.

4. Edit chapter7\urls.py to add the main view to the application, as shown in **Listing** 7.7.

5. Save urls.py.

✔ Tip

■ In Python, code indentation counts, so be sure to indent properly.

Creating the Main Template

The template is the part of the application responsible for rendering the Web page—and the template is the part of the application that we wish to apply our style sheets to.

We'll start by creating the template itself and then make sure our users application is working before going on and creating our style sheet and applying it to the template.

To create the template:

1. Open a command prompt and change to the chapter7 directory:

   `$ cd \django-1.1\django\bin\chapter7`

2. Create a new directory to hold our templates, naming the directory templates:

   `$ md templates`

3. Using a text editor, create the template chapter7\templates\main_page.html and add the contents shown in **Listing 7.8**.

4. Save main_page.html.

5. Edit chapter7\settings.py to add the templates directory to the application (**Listing 7.9**).

```
<html>
  <head>
    <title>
      The users application
    </title>
  </head>
  <body>
    <h1>
      The users application
    </h1>
    <p>
      This is the users application     </p>
  </body>
</html>
```

Listing 7.8 The main_page.html file.

```
TEMPLATE_DIRS = (
    # Put strings here, like   "/home/html/
        django_templates" or   "C:/www/
        django/templates".
    # Always use forward slashes, even on
        Windows.
    # Don't forget to use absolute paths,
        not relative paths.
    "C:/django/Django- 1.1/django/bin/
        chapter7/templates "
```

Listing 7.9 The completed settings.py file.

6. Save settings.py.

Now we'll test the application so far.

7. In the command prompt window, navigate to the chapter7 directory:

```
$ cd django-1.1\django\bin\chapter7
```

8. Run the development server:

```
$ python manage.py runserve6
```

9. Navigate your browser to http://localhost:8000.

You should see the Web page shown in **Figure 7.1**.

That completes the main view. Now we'll create the user view.

Figure 7.1 Starting our users application.

Creating the User View

In the user view, we'll check whether the user is registered in our database, and if the user is registered, we'll greet the user by name:

```
try:
  user =   User.objects.
      get(username=usernam  e)
  message = "Welcome, " + username
      .
      .
      .
```

If the user is not registered, we'll indicate that fact with a different message:

```
try:
  user =   User.objects.
      get(username=usernam e)
  message = "Welcome, " + username
except:
  message = "You are not a registered
      user."
```

The message will be passed to the template for display to the user.

```
from django.http import HttpResponse
from django.contrib.auth.models import User
from django.template import Context
from django.template.loader import
    get_template


def main_page(request):
  template =   get_template('main_page.html')
  variables = Context({
  })
  output = template.render(variables)
  return HttpResponse(output)


def user_page(request, username):
  try:
    user = User.objects.
        get(username=usernam e)
    message = "Welcome, " + username
  except:
    message = "You are not a registered
        user."

  template =   get_template('user_page.html')
  variables = Context({
    'message': message
  })

  output = template.render(variables)
  return HttpResponse(output)
```

Listing 7.10 The completed views.py file.

```
from django.conf.urls.defaults import *
from users.views import *

# Uncomment the next two lines to enable
    the admin:
# from django.contrib import admin
# admin.autodiscover()

urlpatterns = patterns('',
  (r'^$', main_page),
  (r'^(\w+)/$', user_page)
)
```

Listing 7.11 The completed urls.py file.

To create the user view:

1. Using a text editor, edit chapter7\users\ views.py.

2. Add the code to verify the user, shown in **Listing 7.10**.

3. Save views.py.

4. Add user_page to urls.py (**Listing 7.11**).

5. Save urls.py.

Creating the User Template

In the user template, we just want to display the message we created in the user_page view. That message indicates whether the user is a registered user, based on the username.

If the username, as given in the URL that the user enters, is found in the database, the user template will welcome the user by name. If the username is not among the registered users, the message displayed by the template will inform the user that he or she is not a registered user.

To create the user template:

1. Using a text editor, create the user_page. html document in the templates directory, adding the contents shown in **Listing 7.12**.

2. Add the <head> section to the template (**Listing 7.13**).

3. Add the <body> section to the user template (**Listing 7.14**).

   The <body> section is where the message received from the user_page view will appear.

```
<html>
        .
        .
        .
</html>
```

Listing 7.12 Starting user_page.html.

```
<html>
    <head>
        <title>User pages</title>
    </head>
        .
        .
        .
</html>
```

Listing 7.13 Adding the <head> section.

```
<html>
    <head>
        <title>User pages</title>
    </head>
    <body>
        <h1>User pages</h1>
        {{ message }}
    </body>
</html>
```

Listing 7.14 The completed template.

4. Save user_page.html.

5. Open a command prompt and navigate to the chapter7 directory:

```
$ cd django-1.1\django\bin\chapter7
```

6. Run the development server:

```
$ python manage.py runserver
```

7. Navigate your browser to http://localhost:8000/*username*, where *username* is any person's name.

You can see whether the person is a registered user (**Figure 7.2**).

Figure 7.2 A user's page.

Creating a Base Template

Now we'll create a base template, base.html, that will serve as the template from which the main page and the user page will inherit.

The base template typically contains the actual HTML that you want displayed in the browser and lists placeholders for additional content that can be specified by the templates that inherit the base.

For example, a section of the base template might look like this:

```
<html>
  <head>
    <title>
      {% block title %}{% endblock %}
    </title>
</head>
```

In this case, the HTML will appear in the browser with a placeholder for content named title. In the templates that inherit this one, you supply the actual content for the title block. So the base template provides a skeleton template with placeholders that are filled in in the templates that inherit it.

To create a base template:

1. Using a text editor, create chapter7\templates\base.html, adding the code shown in **Listing 7.15**.

   This code provides the HTML framework for our templates.

2. Using a text editor, add the placeholders for two blocks named title and content to the base template (**Listing 7.16**).

   These placeholders will be filled in in templates that inherit from this one.

3. Save base.html.

```
<html>
  <head>
    <title>
      .
      .
      .
    </title>
</head>

  <body>
    <h1>Welcome to the users
    application</h1>
      .
      .
      .
  </body>
</html>
```

Listing 7.15 The edited base.html file.

```
<html>
  <head>
    <title>
      {% block title %}{% endblock %}
    </title>
</head>

  <body>
    <h1>Welcome to the users
    application</h1>
    {% block content %}{% endblock %}
  </body>
</html>
```

Listing 7.16 The completed base.html file.

```
{% extends "base.html" %}

{% block title %}
  Welcome to the users application
{% endblock %}

{% block content %}
  Navigate to http://
localhost:8000/<i>username</i> where
    <i>username</i> is your user name.
{% endblock %}
```

Listing 7.17 The edited main_page.html file.

Inheriting in the Main Template

We have a base template. Now other templates can inherit that template, with the placeholders filled in with customized content.

To make a template inherit a base template, use this syntax, which indicates that the present template is inheriting base.html:

```
{% extends "base.html" %}
```

Then you can specify what content you want in the placeholders in the base template. For example, here's how to fill in the title placeholder:

```
{% extends "base.html" %}

{% block title %}
  Welcome to the users application
{% endblock %}
```

The content you enter for the title block will replace the placeholder for that block in the base template.

When the current template inherits a base template, you typically don't enter any HTML in the current template; you just provide the content that is to replace the placeholders in the base template.

To inherit in the main template:

1. Using a text editor, edit chapter7\templates\main_page.html, replacing the current content with the code shown in **Listing 7.17**.

This code indicates that this template is inheriting base.html.

continues on next page

2. Using a text editor, add the code shown in **Listing 7.18**.

   This code supplies content for the place-holders in the base template.

3. Save main_page.html.

4. Open a command prompt and navigate to the chapter7 directory:

   ```
   $ cd django-1.1\django\bin\chapter7
   ```

5. Run the development server:

   ```
   $ python manage.py runserver
   ```

6. Navigate your browser to http://localhost:8000.

   You should see the Web page shown in **Figure 7.3**. The template displays the base template with content added where the placeholders were.

```
{% extends "base.html" %}

{% block title %}
  Welcome to the users application
{% endblock %}

{% block content %}
  Navigate to http://
localhost:8000/<i>username</i> where
      <i>username</i> is your user name.
{% endblock %}
```

Listing 7.18 The completed main_page.html file.

Figure 7.3 Displaying the main template.

```
{% extends "base.html" %}
        .
        .
        .
```

Listing 7.19 The edited user_page.html file.

```
{% extends "base.html" %}

{% block title %}
  Welcome to the users application
{% endblock %}

{% block content %}
  {{ message }}
```

Listing 7.20 The edited user_page.html file.

Inheriting in the User Template

In this task, we'll make the user_page template inherit the base template and add its own content to the placeholders in the base template.

This template will look much like the main template—and that's the main idea. Template inheritance allows you to create many similar templates without having to create each one from scratch.

In this case, all we have to do is display the message passed to us by the user_page view and fill in the title and content placeholders provided in the base template.

To inherit in the user template:

1. Using a text editor, edit chapter7\
   templates\userpage.html, replacing
   the current content with the code
   shown in **Listing 7.19**.

   This code indicates that this template
   is inheriting base.html.

2. Using a text editor, add the code shown in
   Listing 7.20 to user_page.html.

   This code supplies content for the placeholders and displays the message passed
   from the user view. Notice how sparse the
   user_page template is now.

3. Save user_page.html.

   continues on next page

4. Open a command prompt and navigate to the chapter7 directory:

   `$ cd django-1.1\django\bin\chapter7`

5. Run the development server:

   `$ python manage.py runserver`

6. Navigate your browser to http://localhost:8000/*username*, where *username* is the name of a user in the database.

   You should see a Web page much like the one in **Figure 7.4**.

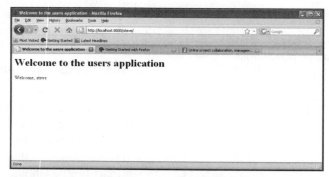

Figure 7.4 Inheriting the user template from the base template.

Changing the Base Template

One of the most useful aspects of template inheritance is that to change all your templates, you have to change only the base template. For example, to change the greeting in your templates from "Welcome to the users application" to "Hello from the users application," you would need to change only this line in the base template:

```
<html>
  <head>
    <title>
      {% block title %}{% endblock %}
    </title>
</head>

  <body>
    <h1>Welcome to the users
    application</h1>
    {% block content %}{% endblock %}
  </body>
</html>
```

You would replace the line with this:

```
<html>
  <head>
    <title>
      {% block title %}{% endblock %}
    </title>
</head>

  <body>
    <h1>Hello from the users
    application</h1>
    {% block content %}{% endblock %}
  </body>
</html>
```

The one change would change all your templates that inherited from the base template.

We'll make that same change here to see how easily you can change all your templates at once by editing the base template.

To change the base template:

1. Using a text editor, open chapter7\templates\base.html (**Listing 7.21**).

2. Using a text editor, change the line of code shown in **Listing 7.22**.

   After you make this change, the change will be reflected in all templates that inherit from this one.

3. Save base.html.

```
<html>
  <head>
    <title>
      {% block title %}{% endblock %}
    </title>
  </head>

  <body>
    <h1>Welcome to the users
    application</h1>
    {% block content %}{% endblock %}
  </body>
</html>
```

Listing 7.21 The current base.html file.

```
<html>
  <head>
    <title>
      {% block title %}{% endblock %}
    </title>
  </head>

  <body>
    <h1>Hello from the users
    application</h1>
    {% block content %}{% endblock %}
  </body>
</html>
```

Listing 7.22 The completed base.html file.

4. Open a command prompt and navigate to the chapter7 directory:

$ `cd django-1.1\django\bin\chapter7`

5. Run the development server:

$ `python manage.py runserver`

6. Navigate your browser to http://localhost:8000/.

You should see the Web page that appears in **Figure 7.5**, showing the main template and reflecting the change you made to the base template.

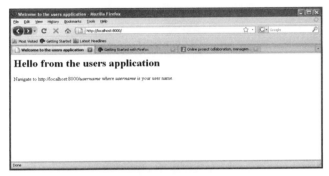

Figure 7.5 Changing the base template.

GETTING USER INPUT: DJANGO FORMS

8

A major part of Web applications is getting information from the user. The user enters data into controls such as text fields and list boxes, and you read that data. That's where this chapter comes in. We're going to display a Web form that lets the user enter data. Then we'll read that data and even save it to disk (making it persistent) by storing that data in our database.

In particular, we'll create a Web form that lets the user enter his or her name and favorite type of ice cream. Then we'll read that data and save it in the data store. To do that, we'll create a Django form, which lets us specify the controls we want to display—here, we want two text fields:

```
from django import forms
```

After creating the form object, we'll pass it to a template using the handy render_to_response() method:

```
form = UserForm()

variables = RequestContext(request, {
  'form': form
})
 return render_to_response('icecream.html', variables)
```

continues on next page

In the template, we'll draw the form using the Django-created data item form.as_p:

```
<html>
  <head>
    <title>Getting user input</title>
  </head>
  <body>
    <h1>Getting user input</h1>
    <form method="post" action=".">
      {{ form.as_p }}
      <input type="submit"
          value="Submit" />
    </form>
  </body>
</html>
```

That draws the form in the browser. After the user enters data, we'll access this data with code in the view, accessing our data from the Django-created cleaned_data array:

```
form = UserForm(request.POST)
if form.is_valid():
  username=
      form.cleaned_data['username'],
  icecream=
      form.cleaned_data['icecream']
```

Then we'll store our data in the model, which is set up to store records named Record, with username and icecream fields, defined this way in models.py:

```
from django.db import models

class Record(models.Model):
  username =
      models.CharField(max_length=200)
  icecream =
      models.CharField(max_length=200)
```

After we create a new record, we'll save it in the model so the user's ice cream selection is stored in our database.

```
INSTALLED_APPS = (
    'django.contrib.auth',
    'django.contrib.contenttypes',
    'django.contrib.sessions',
    'django.contrib.sites',
)
```

Listing 8.1 The settings.py file.

```
INSTALLED_APPS = (
    'django.contrib.auth',
    'django.contrib.contenttypes',
    'django.contrib.sessions',
    'django.contrib.sites',
    'chapter8.forms',)
```

Listing 8.2 The edited settings.py file.

Creating the Project and Application

We'll start creating Django forms by creating a project and application from which to run code. The project will be named chapter8 and the application will be named forms.

To create the chapter8 project and application:

1. To create the Django project, use django-admin.py; open a command prompt and change to the directory that contains that application:

$ cd Django-1.1\django\bin

2. Run django-admin.py, telling it you want to start a new project named chapter8:

$ python django-admin.py
    startproject chapter8

The django-admin.py program creates a new directory named chapter8 under the current directory.

3. Change to the chapter8 directory:

$ cd chapter8

4. Run the manage.py program to create the new application named forms:

$ python manage.py startapp forms

5. Tell Django about your new application, forms; open settings.py in the chapter8 project's directory and find the INSTALLED_APPS section (**Listing 8.1**).

6. Add a line to tell Django about the chapter8.forms application, as shown in **Listing 8.2**.

7. Save the file.

Now we have a new project, chapter8, and a new application, forms. The next step is to create the database.

Creating the Model

The model will hold the usernames and ice cream choices. In particular, we'll create a record type named Record and define the fields like this in models.py:

```
from django.db import models

class Record(models.Model):
  username =
    models.CharField(max_length=200)
  icecream =
    models.CharField(max_length=200)
```

To create the database:

1. Using a text-editing program, open chapter8\settings.py and find the database section (**Listing 8.3**).

2. Enter **'sqlite3'** for the DATABASE_ENGINE setting and **formsdb** for the DATABASE_ NAME setting (**Listing 8.4**).

3. Save settings.py.

✔ Tip

■ In Python, code indentation counts, so be sure to indent properly.

```
DATABASE_ENGINE = ''            #
    'postgresql_psycopg2',
    'postgresql', 'mysql', 'sqlite3'
    or 'oracle'.
DATABASE_NAME = ''              # Or path
    to database file if using
    sqlite3.
DATABASE_USER = ''              # Not used
    with sqlite3.
DATABASE_PASSWORD = ''          # Not used
    with sqlite3.
```

Listing 8.3 The settings.py file.

```
DATABASE_ENGINE = 'sqlite3'         #
    'postgresql_psycopg2',
    'postgresql', 'mysql', 'sqlite3'
    or 'oracle'.
DATABASE_NAME = 'formsdb'           #
    Or path
    to database file if using
    sqlite3.
DATABASE_USER = ''              # Not used
    with sqlite3.
DATABASE_PASSWORD = ''          # Not used
    with sqlite3.
```

Listing 8.4 The edited settings.py file.

```
from django.db import models

class Record(models.Model):
    username = models.CharField(max_length=200)
    icecream = models.CharField(max_length=200)
```

Listing 8.5 The models.py file.

4. Edit chapter8\forms\models.py, using the code in **Listing 8.5** as the entire contents of models.py.

5. Save models.py.

6. Open a command prompt, and in the chapter8 directory, enter this command to set up the database system:

   `$ python manage.py syncdb`

7. When prompted to create a superuser for the database, enter this data:

   You just installed Django's auth system, which means you don't have any superusers defined.
   Would you like to create one now? (yes/no):

   Enter **yes**.

   Username:

   Enter a name.

   E-mail address:

   Enter an email address.

   Password:

   Enter a password.

   Password (again):

   Enter the password again.

   The database is now set up.

Creating the Form

Now we're going to create the form that contains the controls in which the user will enter data. In this case, we'll have two text fields: one for the user's name and one for the name of the user's favorite ice cream flavor.

Django forms are based on the `django import forms` class. We'll import that class and then create our own class from it, named `UserForm`, in a file named forms.py:

```
from django import forms

class UserForm(forms.Form):
  username = forms.
    CharField(label='Username',
    max_length=30)
  icecream = forms.CharField(label='Ice
    cream', max_length=30)
```

To create the form:

1. Using a text editor, create the document chapter8\forms\forms.py and enter the code shown in **Listing 8.6** to import the Django forms support.

2. Add the code to create our new `UserForm` class (**Listing 8.7**).

3. Add the code to add the two text fields and their labels to the form (**Listing 8.8**).

4. Save forms.py.

We've created the class we'll use for our forms, UserForm, in forms.py.

```
from django import forms

        .
        .
        .
```

Listing 8.6 Starting forms.py.

```
from django import forms

class UserForm(forms.Form):

        .
        .
        .
```

Listing 8.7 Editing forms.py.

```
from django import forms

class UserForm(forms.Form):
    username = forms.CharField(label='Username',
        max_length=30)
    icecream = forms.CharField(label='Ice
        cream', max_length=30)
```

Listing 8.8 Completing forms.py.

```
from django.http import HttpResponse
from django.template import RequestContext
from django.shortcuts import
    render_to_response
from forms import *
from models import *
def main_page(request):
  if request.method == 'POST':
      .
      .
      .

  else:
      .
      .
      .
```

Listing 8.9 The views.py file.

```
from django.http import HttpResponse
from django.template import RequestContext
from django.shortcuts import
    render_to_response
from forms import *
from models import *
def main_page(request):
  if request.method == 'POST':
      .
      .
      .

  else:
    form = UserForm()
      .
      .
      .
```

Listing 8.10 The edited views.py file.

Creating the View That Displays the Form

Next we'll create the forms application main view, which will display the form. We need to check whether the form has already been displayed, and if it hasn't, we want it displayed so the user can enter data. If the form has been displayed, we need to read the user data from it.

To find out whether the form has already been displayed, we'll code the form to be sent to the server using the POST method. Then, if the request method was POST, we'll know that the form has already been displayed. If the request method was not POST, we'll know that we need to display the form. Our view will be called main_page.

To create the view that displays the form:

1. Using a text editor, edit chapter8\forms\ views.py, adding the code shown in **Listing 8.9** to check whether the request method was POST. (The final version of this file appears in Listing 8.19.)

2. Add the code shown in **Listing 8.10** to create a new UserForm object if the request method was not POST (which means that the form has not yet been displayed).

continues on next page

3. Add the code to render the form by passing it to the template using the `render_to_response` method (**Listing 8.11**).

4. Save views.py.

5. Edit chapter8\urls.py, adding the main_page view URL to the urlpatterns section (**Listing 8.12**).

6. Save urls.py.

```python
from django.http import HttpResponse
from django.template import RequestContext
from django.shortcuts import
    render_to_response
from forms import *
from models import *
def main_page(request):
  if request.method == 'POST':
        .
        .
        .
  else:
    form = UserForm()

  variables = RequestContext(request, {
    'form': form
  })
    return render_to_response(
      'icecream.html', variables)
```

Listing 8.11 The completed views.py file.

```python
from django.conf.urls.defaults import *
from forms.views import *

urlpatterns = patterns('',
  (r'^$', main_page),
)
```

Listing 8.12 The urls.py file.

```
<html>
  <head>
    <title>Getting user input</title>
  </head>
  <body>
    <h1>Getting user input</h1>
        .
        .
        .
  </body>
</html>
```

Listing 8.13 The icecream.html file.

Creating the Template

The template in this application is named icecream.html, and its job is to display the form that contains the two text fields.

The view will pass the form to the template, so the template needs only to set up an HTML form element and then render the Django form in it. You do that with the Django data member `form.as_p` in icecream.html:

```
<form method="post" action=".">
  {{ form.as_p }}
  <input type="submit" value="Submit"
  />
</form>
```

That draws the form, displaying the two text fields to the user.

To create the template:

1. Open a command prompt and change to the chapter8 directory:

   `$ cd \django-1.1\django\bin\chapter8`

2. Create a new directory to hold our templates and name the directory templates:

   `$ md templates`

3. Using a text editor, create the template chapter8\templates\icecream.html and add the contents shown in **Listing 8.13**.

continues on next page

4. Add the code shown in **Listing 8.14** to render the Django form we've created.

5. Save icecream.html.

   That completes the template.

6. Add the new templates directory to the TEMPLATE_DIRS section of settings.py (**Listing 8.15**).

7. Save settings.py.

```html
<html>
  <head>
    <title>Getting user input</title>
  </head>
  <body>
    <h1>Getting user input</h1>
    <form method="post" action=".">
      {{ form.as_p }}
      <input type="submit" value="Submit"
      />
    </form>
  </body>
</html>
```

Listing 8.14 The completed icecream.html file.

```python
TEMPLATE_DIRS = (
"C:/django/Django-1.1/django/bin/chapter8/
    templates"
)
```

Listing 8.15 The settings.py file.

```
from django.http import HttpResponse
from django.template import RequestContext
from django.shortcuts import
    render_to_response
from forms import *
from models import *

def main_page(request):
  if request.method == 'POST':
    form = UserForm(request.POST)
    if form.is_valid():
        .
        .
        .
  else:
    form = UserForm()

  variables = RequestContext(request, {
    'form': form
  })
    return render_to_response(
      'icecream.html', variables)
```

Listing 8.16 The edited views.py file.

Creating the View That Displays the Results

After the form has been displayed, it will be returned to the view. We'll know that there is data waiting for us in the form because the request method will be set to POST (the default is GET, but we set the request method to POST in the form itself). When we get the filled-out form back, we can extract the user's name and ice cream flavor from it.

To create the view that displays the results:

1. Using a text editor, edit chapter8\forms\views.py.

2. Add the code to check on the user (**Listing 8.16**).

    Here, we get the form and check its is_valid() method, which fills the cleaned_data array with the data we're going to extract.

    continues on next page

3. Add the code to extract the username and ice cream flavor from the form (**Listing 8.17**).

4. Save views.py.

We have recovered the username and ice cream flavor from the form. The next step is to display that information.

✔ Tip

■ You'll learn more about checking the validity of forms in the next chapter.

```
from django.http import HttpResponse
from django.template import RequestContext
from django.shortcuts import
    render_to_response
from forms import *
from models import *

def main_page(request):
  if request.method == 'POST':
    form = UserForm(request.POST)
    if form.is_valid():
      username=form.cleaned_data[
        'username'],
      icecream=form.cleaned_data[
        'icecream']
        .
        .
        .
    else:
      form = UserForm()

  variables = RequestContext(request, {
    'form': form
  })
    return render_to_response(
      'icecream.html', variables)
    return render_to_response(
      'icecream.html', variables)
```

Listing 8.17 The completed views.py file.

```
from django.http import HttpResponse
from django.template import RequestContext
from django.shortcuts import
    render_to_response
from forms import *
from models import *


def main_page(request):
  if request.method == 'POST':
    form = UserForm(request.POST)
    if form.is_valid():
      username=form.cleaned_data[
        'username'],
      icecream=form.cleaned_data[
        'icecream']
    output = '''
    <html>
      <head>
        <title>
          Reading user data
        </title>
      </head>
      <body>
        <h1>
          Reading user data
        </h1>
        Your ice cream is: %s
      </body>
    </html>''' % (
        icecream
    )
    return HttpResponse(output)
  else:
    form = UserForm()

  variables = RequestContext(request, {
    'form': form
  })
    return render_to_response(
      'icecream.html', variables)
```

Listing 8.18 The edited views.py file.

Displaying the Data Read from the Form

We've recovered the user's name and ice cream flavor from the form. Now we'll display the ice cream flavor that the user entered. To save time, we'll do this directly from the view, without a template.

To display the data:

1. Using a text editor, edit chapter8\forms\ views.py.

2. Add the code shown in **Listing 8.18**. This code will display the ice cream flavor that the user entered.

3. Save views.py.

Now we have all the parts in place: urls.py, settings.py, views.py, icecream.html, and models.py. In the next task, we'll put the form to the test.

Testing the Form

It's time to test the form by entering some data and seeing whether the application can read that data and echo it to the browser.

You'll first navigate to the main page, which should display the form: two text fields with labels. You'll then enter your name in the Username field and your favorite ice cream flavor in the Ice Cream field and click the Submit button. The application should get the form and read the data in it, displaying your favorite ice cream flavor.

To test the form:

1. Open a command prompt and navigate to the chapter8 directory:

   ```
   $ cd django-1.1\django\bin\chapter8
   ```

2. Run the development server:

   ```
   $ python manage.py runserver
   ```

3. Navigate your browser to http://localhost:8000.

4. Enter your name in the Username text field.

5. Enter the ice cream flavor you prefer in the Ice Cream text field.

   Your Web page should look similar to **Figure 8.1**.

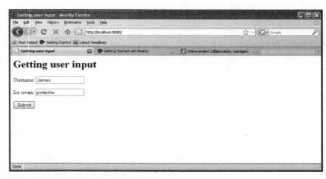

Figure 8.1 The form in a Web page.

6. Click the Submit button.

You should see a Web page similar to the one in **Figure 8.2**, displaying the ice cream flavor that you entered.

This application works because we were able to recover the username and ice cream flavor from the cleans_data array and display the data to the user:

```
if request.method == 'POST':
  form = UserForm(request.POST)
  if form.is_valid():
    username=form.cleaned_data[
      'username'],
    icecream=form.cleaned_data[
      'icecream']
  output = '''
<html>
  <head>
    <title>
      Reading user data
    </title>
  </head>
  <body>
    <h1>
      Reading user data
    </h1>
    Your ice cream is: %s
  </body>
</html>''' % (
  icecream
)
return HttpResponse(output)
```

Figure 8.2
Displaying the ice cream flavor.

Making Form Data Persistent

So far, we've been reading data from the user. How can we store that data on a disk? With the model, of course—the model is all about saving application data, or making it persistent.

In this task, we'll store the user's name and ice cream flavor in a database record. We've already set up the model with records named Record to store such data:

```
from django.db import models
class Record(models.Model):
    username =
        models.CharField(max_length=200)
    icecream =
        models.CharField(max_length=200)
```

To make form data persistent:

1. Using a text editor, edit chapter8\forms\ views.py.

2. Add the code shown in **Listing 8.19**. This code will create and save a new record of type Record in the model.

3. Save views.py.

4. Open a command prompt and navigate to the chapter8 directory:

    ```
    $ cd django-1.1\django\bin\chapter8
    ```

```python
from django.http import HttpResponse
from django.template import RequestContext
from django.shortcuts import
    render_to_response
from forms import *
from models import *

def main_page(request):
  if request.method == 'POST':
    form = UserForm(request.POST)
    if form.is_valid():
      username=form.cleaned_data[
        'username'],
      icecream=form.cleaned_data[
        'icecream']
      record = Record(
        username = form.cleaned_data[
          'username'],
        icecream = form.cleaned_data[
          'icecream']
      )
      record.save()
    output = '''
    <html>
      <head>
        <title>
          Reading user data
        </title>
      </head>
      <body>
        <h1>
          Reading user data
        </h1>
        Your ice cream is: %s
      </body>
    </html>''' % (
        icecream
    )
    return HttpResponse(output)
  else:
    form = UserForm()

  variables = RequestContext(request, {
    'form': form
  })
    return render_to_response(
      'icecream.html', variables)
```

Listing 8.19 The completed views.py file.

5. Run the development server:

```
$ python manage.py runserver
```

6. Navigate your browser to http://localhost:8000.

7. Enter your name in the Username text field.

8. Enter the ice cream flavor you prefer in the Ice Cream text field.

9. Click the Submit button.

The application should echo the ice cream flavor.

Your data should be persistent in the model. We'll verify that in the next task.

Verifying Persistent Data

You've entered your data in the form and clicked Submit—and the application seemed to do what it was supposed to do. But is your data actually persistent?

In this task, we'll verify that the data you entered was recorded in the database. To do that we'll use the shell you start with manage.py.

To verify that your data is persistent:

1. Open a command prompt and navigate to the chapter8 directory:

   ```
   $ cd django-1.1\django\bin\chapter8
   ```

2. Run the shell:

   ```
   $ python manage.py shell
   ```

   You should see code similar to **Listing 8.20**.

3. At the >>> prompt, import the model we're using (**Listing 8.21**).

```
C:\Django\Django-1.1\django\bin\
      chapter8>c:\python26\python manage.p
Python 2.6.1 (r261:67517, Dec  4 2008,
      16:51:00) [MSC v.1500 32 bit
win32
Type "help", "copyright", "credits" or
      "license" for more information
(InteractiveConsole)
>>>
```

Listing 8.20 The Django shell.

```
C:\Django\Django-1.1\django\bin\
      chapter8>c:\python26\python manage.p
Python 2.6.1 (r261:67517, Dec  4 2008,
      16:51:00) [MSC v.1500 32 bit
win32
Type "help", "copyright", "credits" or
      "license" for more information
(InteractiveConsole)
>>> from forms.models import *
```

Listing 8.21 Using the shell.

```
C:\Django\Django-1.1\django\bin\
      chapter8>c:\python26\python manage.p
Python 2.6.1 (r261:67517, Dec  4 2008,
      16:51:00) [MSC v.1500 32 bit
win32
Type "help", "copyright", "credits" or
      "license" for more information
(InteractiveConsole)
>>> from forms.models import *
>>> Record.objects.get(id=1).username
u'James'
>>> Record.objects.get(id=1).icecream
u'pistachio'
```

Listing 8.22 Examining a record.

```
C:\Django\Django-1.1\django\bin\
      chapter8>c:\python26\python manage.p
Python 2.6.1 (r261:67517, Dec  4 2008,
      16:51:00) [MSC v.1500 32 bit
win32
Type "help", "copyright", "credits" or
      "license" for more information
(InteractiveConsole)
>>> from forms.models import *
>>> Record.objects.get(id=1).username
u'James'
>>> Record.objects.get(id=1).icecream
u'pistachio'
>>>exit()
```

Listing 8.23 Exiting the shell.

4. At the >>> prompt, examine the first record's username and ice cream flavor to confirm that they hold the data you entered (**Listing 8.22**).

Great—your data is in the database.

5. At the >>> prompt, exit the shell (**Listing 8.23**).

VERIFYING PERSISTENT DATA

VALIDATING FORM DATA

In the previous chapter, we read data entered by the user with Web forms that display controls such as text fields. In this chapter, we'll see how to check that data—that is, validate it—before working with it.

For example, you may have an application that lets you create new users on the fly if people enter a username, email address, and password. As this chapter shows, you can check to make sure that the email address is valid before accepting it. You can also ask the user to enter the password twice and then verify that the two entries match before accepting the password. Similarly, you can check to make sure that the username a new user specifies doesn't already exist in your application.

To validate data items that have been named in the form, you create a clean_*item()* function, where *item* is the name of the data item you're checking; this function will be called automatically by Django. So, for example, to compare two passwords, named password1 and password2, you can define the function clean_password2():

```
def clean_password2(self):
    .
    .
    .
```

If the user enters a value for the data item, that item will be available in the self. cleaned_data array, so to check that, enter:

```
def clean_password2(self):
    if 'password1' in self.cleaned_data:
        .
        .
        .
```

continues on next page

If the item exists, you can access it, like this for the first password:

```
def clean_password2(self):
  if 'password1' in self.cleaned_data:
    password1 =
     self.cleaned_data['password1']
    .
    .
    .
```

To access password2, the second password that the user entered, which should match password1, you enter:

```
def clean_password2(self):
  if 'password1' in self.cleaned_data:
    password1 =
     self.cleaned_data['password1']
  if 'password2' in self.cleaned_data:
    password2 =
     self.cleaned_data['password2']
    .
    .
    .
```

Then you can check whether the two passwords match, and if so, return the accepted password:

```
def clean_password2(self):
  if 'password1' in self.cleaned_data:
    password1 =
     self.cleaned_data['password1']
  if 'password2' in self.cleaned_data:
    password2 =
     self.cleaned_data['password2']
    if password1 == password2:
     return password2
    .
    .
    .
```

If the passwords don't match, you can return an error message or raise an exception:

```
def clean_password2(self):
  if 'password1' in self.cleaned_data:
    password1 =
     self.cleaned_data['password1']
  if 'password2' in self.cleaned_data:
    password2 =
     self.cleaned_data['password2']
    if password1 == password2:
      return password2
  return 'no good!'
```

The view will be able to access the value you've stored for password2—which may be an error message—after the validation is complete.

Let's put validation to work now in an application that lets you create new users.

Creating the Project and Application

To see how to validate Django forms, we'll first create a project and application from which to run code. The project will be chapter9 and the application will be named forms.

To create the chapter9 project and application:

1. To create the Django project, use django-admin.py: open a command prompt and change to the directory that contains that application:

   ```
   $ cd Django-1.1\django\bin
   ```

2. Run django-admin.py, telling it that you want to start a new project named chapter9:

   ```
   $ python django-admin.py
      startproject chapter9
   ```

   The django-admin.py program creates a new directory named chapter9 under the current directory.

3. Change to the chapter9 directory:

   ```
   $ cd chapter9
   ```

4. Run the manage.py program to create the new application named forms:

   ```
   $ python manage.py startapp forms
   ```

5. Tell Django about your new application, forms: open settings.py in the chapter9 project's directory and find the INSTALLED_APPS section (**Listing 9.1**).

6. Add a line to tell Django about the chapter9.forms application as shown in **Listing 9.2**.

7. Save the file.

Now we have a new project, chapter9, and a new application, forms. The next step is to create the database that contains the user data.

```
INSTALLED_APPS = (
    'django.contrib.auth',
    'django.contrib.contenttypes',
    'django.contrib.sessions',
    'django.contrib.sites',
)
```

Listing 9.1 The settings.py file.

```
INSTALLED_APPS = (
    'django.contrib.auth',
    'django.contrib.contenttypes',
    'django.contrib.sessions',
    'django.contrib.sites',
    'chapter9.forms',)
```

Listing 9.2 The edited settings.py file.

```
DATABASE_ENGINE = ''          #
    'postgresql_psycopg2',
    'postgresql', 'mysql', 'sqlite3'
    or 'oracle'.
DATABASE_NAME = ''            # Or path
    to database file if using
    sqlite3.
DATABASE_USER = ''            # Not used
    with sqlite3.
DATABASE_PASSWORD = ''        # Not used
    with sqlite3.
```

Listing 9.3 The settings.py file.

```
DATABASE_ENGINE = 'sqlite3'       #
    'postgresql_psycopg2',
    'postgresql', 'mysql', 'sqlite3'
    or 'oracle'.
DATABASE_NAME = 'formsdb'         #
    Or path
    to database file if using
    sqlite3.
DATABASE_USER = ''               # Not used
    with sqlite3.
DATABASE_PASSWORD = ''           # Not used
    with sqlite3.
```

Listing 9.4 The edited settings.py file.

Creating the Database

The model will hold the data that new users enter. Here's what models.py looks like now:

```
from django.db import models
```

```
# Create your models here.
```

And here's what it will look like after this task is complete:

```
from django.db import models
```

```
from django.contrib.auth.models import
    User
```

To create the database:

1. Using a text-editing program, open chapter9\settings.py and find the database section (**Listing 9.3**).

2. Enter **'sqlite3'** for the DATABASE_ENGINE setting and **formsdb** for the DATABASE_ NAME setting (**Listing 9.4**).

3. Save settings.py.

✔ Tip

■ In Python, code indentation counts, so be sure to indent properly.

continues on next page

4. Edit chapter9\forms\models.py and use the code in **Listing 9.5** as the entire contents of models.py.

5. Save models.py.

6. Open a command prompt, and in the chapter9 directory, enter this command to set up the database system:

```
$ python manage.py syncdb
```

7. When prompted to create a superuser for the database, enter this data:

You just installed Django's auth system, which means you don't have any superusers defined.

Would you like to create one now? (yes/no):

Enter **yes**.

Username:

Enter a name.

E-mail address:

Enter an email address.

Password:

Enter a password.

Password (again):

Enter the password again.

The database is now set up.

```
from django.db import models

from django.contrib.auth.models import User
```

Listing 9.5 The models.py file.

```
from django import forms
          .
          .
          .
```

Listing 9.6 Starting forms.py.

```
from django import forms

class UserForm(forms.Form):
          .
          .
          .
```

Listing 9.7 Editing forms.py.

```
from django import forms
from models import *

class UserForm(forms.Form):
  username = forms.
    CharField(label='Username',
    max_length=30)
  email = forms.EmailField(label='Email')
  password1 = forms.CharField(
    label='Password',
    widget=forms.PasswordInput()
  )
  password2 = forms.CharField(
    label='Password again',
    widget=forms.PasswordInput()
  )
```

Listing 9.8 Completing forms.py.

Creating the Form

Now we'll create the form to gather new user information. Here, we'll collect the username, the email address, and the password (entered twice to make sure it's been entered correctly).

When you create controls in a form, you can specify the widget used to display the control. For example, here's how to display a password field:

```
password1 = forms.CharField(
  label='Password',
  widget=forms.PasswordInput()
)
```

Here, we're using the forms.PasswordInput() control to create a password control (which masks typed characters with a *).

To create the form:

1. Using a text editor, create the document chapter9\forms\forms.py and enter the code to import the Django forms support (**Listing 9.6**).

2. Add the code shown in **Listing 9.7** to create our new UserForm class.

3. Add the code to add the username, email, and password fields to the form (**Listing 9.8**).

4. Save forms.py.

This creates the class we'll use for our forms, UserForm.

Creating the View That Displays the Form

Next we'll create the forms application main view, which will display the form. We need to check whether the form has already been displayed and, if not, display it. If the form has been displayed, we need to read the user data from it. How do we know whether the form has been displayed? If the request method is POST, the form is being returned from the browser (because we set things up that way in forms.py); if the method is not POST, we need to display the form so the new user can fill in the information.

To create the view that displays the form:

1. Using a text editor, edit chapter9\forms\ views.py, add the code shown in **Listing 9.9** to check whether the request method was POST. If it wasn't, we'll call our main main_page view.

2. Add the code to create a new UserForm object if the request method was not POST, (which means that the form has not yet been displayed; **Listing 9.10**).

```
from django.http import HttpResponse
from django.contrib.auth.models import User
from django.template import RequestContext
from django.shortcuts import
    render_to_response
from forms import *
def main_page(request):
  if request.method == 'POST':
            .
            .
            .
    else:
            .
            .
            .
```

Listing 9.9 The views.py file.

```
from django.http import HttpResponse
from django.contrib.auth.models import User
from django.template import RequestContext
from django.shortcuts import
    render_to_response
from forms import *
def main_page(request):
  if request.method == 'POST':
            .
            .
            .
    else:
        form = UserForm()
```

Listing 9.10 The edited views.py file.

```
from django.http import HttpResponse
from django.contrib.auth.models import User
from django.template import RequestContext
from django.shortcuts import
    render_to_response
from forms import *
def main_page(request):
  if request.method == 'POST':
      .
      .
      .
  else:
    form = UserForm()

  variables = RequestContext(request, {
    'form': form
  })
  return render_to_response('register.html',
    variables)
```

Listing 9.11 The completed views.py file.

```
from django.conf.urls.defaults import *
from forms.views import *

urlpatterns = patterns('',
  (r'^$', main_page),
)
```

Listing 9.12 The urls.py file.

3. Add the code to render the form by passing it to the template using the render_to_response method (**Listing 9.11**).

4. Save views.py.

5. Edit chapter9\urls.py, adding the main_page view URL to the url_patterns section (**Listing 9.12**).

6. Save urls.py.

Creating the Template

The template in this application is named register.html, because it will allow new users to register themselves, and its job is to display the form.

The view will pass the form to the template, so the template has only to set up an HTML form element and then render the Django form in it. You do that with the Django data member form.as_p in register.html:

```
<form method="post" action=".">
  {{ form.as_p }}
  <input type="submit" value="Submit"
  />
</form>
```

To create the template:

1. Open a command prompt and change to the chapter9 directory:

   ```
   $ cd \django-1.1\duango\bin\chapter9
   ```

2. Create a new directory to hold our templates, naming the directory templates:

   ```
   $ md templates
   ```

3. Using a text editor, create the template chapter9\templates\register.html and add the contents shown in **Listing 9.13**.

4. Add the code to render the Django form we've created (**Listing 9.14**).

5. Save register.html.
   That completes the template.

6. Add the new templates directory to the TEMPLATE_DIRS section of settings.py (**Listing 9.15**).

7. Save settings.py.

```
<html>
  <head>
    <title>Sign up as a new user</title>
  </head>
  <body>
    <h1>Sign up as a new user</h1>
          .
          .
          .
  </body>
</html>
```

Listing 9.13 The register.html file.

```
<html>
  <head>
    <title>Sign up as a new user</title>
  </head>
  <body>
    <h1>Sign up as a new user</h1>
    <form method="post" action=".">
      {{ form.as_p }}
      <input type="submit" value="Submit"
      />
    </form>
  </body>
</html>
```

Listing 9.14 The completed register.html file.

```
TEMPLATE_DIRS = (
"C:/django/Django-1.1/django/bin/chapter9/
    templates"
)
```

Listing 9.15 The settings.py file.

```
def main_page(request):
  if request.method == 'POST':
    form = UserForm(request.POST)
    email=''
    if form.is_valid():
      email='Your email is ' +
        form.cleaned_data['email']

    else:
      email='Sorry, that email is not valid'
    output = '''
      <html>
        <head>
          <title>
            Validating data
          </title>
        </head>
        <body>
          <h1>
          Validating data
        </h1>
        %s
        </body>
      </html>''' % (
      email
    )
```

Listing 9.16 The edited views.py file.

Validating the Email Address

We used an `EmailField()` control to get the user's email address in forms.py:

```
class UserForm(forms.Form):
  username = forms.CharField(label=
    'Username', max_length=30)
  email = forms.EmailField(label=
    'Email')
  password1 = forms.CharField(
    label='Password',
    widget=forms.PasswordInput()
  )
  password2 = forms.CharField(
    label='Password again',
    widget=forms.PasswordInput()
  )
```

That control performs its own validation checking. If the email address is not in valid form, the `EmailField()` control throws an exception, and the form's `is_valid()` method returns false.

We'll check the `is_valid()` method in the view, and if its value is false, we'll tell the user that the email address was entered in the wrong format.

To validate the email address:

1. Using a text editor, edit chapter9\forms\ views.py and add the code shown in **Listing 9.16** to check whether the email value threw an exception.

2. Save views.py.

We have checked the email address and displayed an error message if necessary.

Validating the Password

For the password, we just want to make sure that both entered passwords are the same. If they are, we'll return the password; otherwise, we'll return an error message (we could also return an error by raising `forms.ValidationError` in our code).

There are two password entries, password1 and password2, and we'll define a function named `clean_password2()`. This function will be called automatically by Django to validate password2.

To validate the password:

1. Using a text editor, edit chapter9\forms\forms.py and add the code shown in **Listing 9.17** to create the `clean_password2()` function and get the values of the two passwords: password1 and password2.

2. Add the code to check whether the passwords match and, if they do, return a message indicating what the password is (**Listing 9.18**).

3. Add the code to return an error if one occurs (**Listing 9.19**).

4. Save forms.py.

✔ Tip

- The whole forms.py file is shown later in Listing 9.21.

```python
def clean_password2(self):
  if 'password1' in self.cleaned_data:
    password1 =
      self.cleaned_data['password1']
  if 'password2' in self.cleaned_data:
    password2 =
      self.cleaned_data['password2']
    .
    .
    .
```

Listing 9.17 The forms.py file.

```python
def clean_password2(self):
  if 'password1' in self.cleaned_data:
    password1 =
      self.cleaned_data['password1']
  if 'password2' in self.cleaned_data:
    password2 =
      self.cleaned_data['password2']
    if password1 == password2:
      return 'Your password is ' +
          password2
    .
    .
    .
```

Listing 9.18 The edited forms.py file.

```python
def clean_password2(self):
  if 'password1' in self.cleaned_data:
    password1 =
      self.cleaned_data['password1']
  if 'password2' in self.cleaned_data:
    password2 =
      self.cleaned_data['password2']
    if password1 == password2:
      return 'Your password is ' + password2
  return 'Sorry, passwords do not match'
```

Listing 9.19 The new forms.py file.

VALIDATING THE PASSWORD

```
from django import forms
from models import *

class UserForm(forms.Form):
  username =
    forms.CharField(label='Username',
    max_length=30)
  email = forms.EmailField(label='Email')
  password1 = forms.CharField(
    label='Password',
    widget=forms.PasswordInput()
  )
  password2 = forms.CharField(
    label='Password again',
    widget=forms.PasswordInput()
  )

  def clean_username(self):
    username = self.cleaned_data['username']
    try:
      User.objects.get(username=username)
    except:
      return 'Your username is ' + username
      .
      .
      .
```

Listing 9.20 Editing forms.py.

Validating the Username

We can also validate the new username that the user entered by checking the model. If that username is already in use, we should inform the user that the selection is already taken.

We'll check the username in a new function, clean_username(), which will be called by Django automatically because username is one of the fields in the form. We'll return either the new username or, if that username is already taken, an error message.

To validate the username:

1. Using a text editor, edit chapter9\forms\ forms.py and add the code to create the clean_username() function and obtain the username value from usersdb (**Listing 9.20**).

continues on next page

VALIDATING THE USERNAME

2. Add the code to return an error message if one is needed, as shown in **Listing 9.21**, which shows the entire forms.py program.

3. Save forms.py.

```python
from django import forms
from models import *


class UserForm(forms.Form):
  username =
      forms.CharField(label='Username',
      max_length=30)
  email = forms.EmailField(label='Email')
  password1 = forms.CharField(
    label='Password',
    widget=forms.PasswordInput()
  )
  password2 = forms.CharField(
    label='Password again',
    widget=forms.PasswordInput()
  )

  def clean_username(self):
    username = self.cleaned_data['username']
    try:
      User.objects.get(username=username)
    except:
      return 'Your username is ' + username
    return 'Username is already in use'

  def clean_password2(self):
    if 'password1' in self.cleaned_data:
      password1 =
        self.cleaned_data['password1']
    if 'password2' in self.cleaned_data:
      password2 =
        self.cleaned_data['password2']
      if password1 == password2:
        return 'Your password is ' + password2
    return 'Sorry, passwords do not match'
```

Listing 9.21 The completed forms.py file.

```
from django.http import HttpResponse
from django.contrib.auth.models import User
from django.template import RequestContext
from django.shortcuts import
    render_to_response
from forms import *

def main_page(request):
  if request.method == 'POST':
    form = UserForm(request.POST)
    username=''
    password=''
    email=''
    if form.is_valid():
      email='Your email is ' +
        form.cleaned_data['email']
      username=form.cleaned_data['username']
      password=form.cleaned_data['password2']
    else:
      email='Sorry, that email is not valid'
    output = '''
      <html>
        <head>
          <title>
            Validating data
          </title>
        </head>
        <body>
          <h1>
          Validating data
        </h1>
        %s
        <br>
        %s
        <br>
        %s
        </body>
      </html>''' % (
      email,
      username,
      password
    )

    return HttpResponse(output)
  else:
    form = UserForm()

  variables = RequestContext(request, {
    'form': form
  })
  return render_to_response('register.
    html', variables)
```

Listing 9.22 The completed views.py file.

Creating the View That Displays the Results

We've already edited views.py to display an error message if the email address entered by the user isn't in valid format. In this task, we'll also display the username and password messages returned from forms.py.

To create the view that displays the results:

1. Using a text editor, edit chapter9\forms\ views.py.

2. Add the code to display the username and password, or their error messages (**Listing 9.22**).

   This is the completed version of views.py.

3. Save views.py.

Verifying Validation

Now we'll test the validation we've set up to make sure that things are working as we expect. We'll try entering invalid data and see whether the application finds it.

To verify validation:

1. Open a command prompt and change to the chapter9 directory:

   ```
   $ cd django\django-1.1\django\bin\
     chapter9
   ```

2. Run the development server:

   ```
   $ python manage.py runserver
   ```

3. Navigate your browser to http://localhost:8000.

   You should see the page shown in **Figure 9.1**.

4. Enter valid information in the form.

Figure 9.1 The main page of the application.

5. Click the Submit button.

The page that appears should summarize your information, as shown in **Figure 9.2**.

6. Navigate back to http://localhost:8000 and fill out the form again, this time with the username of an existing user.

The username nancy already exists in the database (**Figure 9.3**).

continues on next page

Figure 9.2 The main page showing valid data.

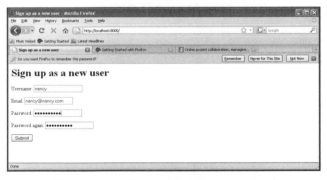

Figure 9.3 The main page with an existing username entered.

7. Click the Submit button.

The application should identify the error and display a message (**Figure 9.4**).

8. Navigate back to http://localhost:8000 and fill out the form again, this time with two passwords that don't match (**Figure 9.5**).

Figure 9.4 Message indicating that the username is already in use.

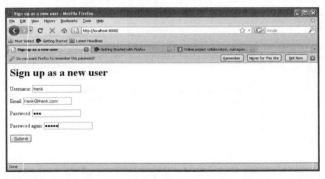

Figure 9.5 The main page with nonmatching passwords.

9. Click the Submit button.

The application should indicate that the passwords don't match (**Figure 9.6**).

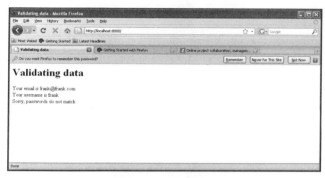

Figure 9.6 Message indicating that the passwords don't match.

LOGGING USERS IN AND OUT

Django lets you keep track of who's logged in on your site, and you can track users from page to page, as you'll see in this chapter. Here, we're going to create an application that lets users log in, greets them by name when they do, and lets them log out.

The application is named login, and it will consist of three pages: a main page that greets users by name if they're logged in or, if they're not logged in, invites them to log in; a login page with text fields for username and password; and a logout page (which is actually not a page at all—it's just a view that logs users out and returns them to the main page).

So when a user opens the application, the user will be invited to log in. When the user logs in, the application will greet the user by name and display a link to let the user log out. When the user clicks the link, the user will be logged out and returned to the main page—which will invite the user to log in again.

To save time, we'll create a base template that displays features common to all the pages, such as the links to the main page and the login page if the user is not yet logged in and the logout page if the user is logged in. Our templates will inherit from that base template.

Django gives us considerable assistance here. It lets us log in users using the `django.contrib.auth.views.login` class: we tie the login URL to this class, provide a template named login.html in a directory named registration within our templates directory, and indicate to Django what page we want displayed after the user logs in, and Django takes care of the rest. It opens a login page in the browser with two text fields—one for the username and one for the password—and if the user successfully logs in, we can access an object named User in our subsequent pages.

continues on next page

To log out the user, we can just call the logout method in the view corresponding to the logout link, and Django will log out the user.

So that's how it works: Django helps us log users in and out, and we can access the User object in our pages to see if the user is logged in (with the `user.is_authenticated` method) and get the user's name (with `user.username`).

Let's put all this to work in a new application named login that lets users log in, greets them by name when they do, and then lets them log out.

```
INSTALLED_APPS = (
    'django.contrib.auth',
    'django.contrib.contenttypes',
    'django.contrib.sessions',
    'django.contrib.sites',
)
```

Listing 10.1 The settings.py file.

```
INSTALLED_APPS = (
    'django.contrib.auth',
    'django.contrib.contenttypes',
    'django.contrib.sessions',
    'django.contrib.sites',
    'chapter10.login',)
```

Listing 10.2 The edited settings.py file.

Creating the Project and Application

We'll start by creating a project and application for our code. The project will be chapter10 and the application will be named login.

To create the chapter10 project and application:

1. Create the Django project using django-admin.py: open a command prompt and change to the directory that contains that application:

    `$ cd Django-1.1\django\bin`

2. Run django-admin.py, telling it you want to start a new project named chapter10:

    `$ python django-admin.py`
    `   startproject chapter10`

    The django-admin.py program creates a new directory named chapter10 under the current directory.

3. Change to the chapter10 directory:

    `$ cd chapter10`

4. Run the manage.py program to create the new application named login:

    `$ python manage.py startapp login`

5. Tell Django about your new application, login: open settings.py in the chapter10 project's directory and find the INSTALLED_APPS section (**Listing 10.1**).

6. Add a line to tell Django about the chapter10.login application, as shown in **Listing 10.2**.

7. Save the file.

Now we have a new project, chapter10, and a new application, login. The next step is to create the database.

CREATING THE PROJECT AND APPLICATION

Creating the Database

In this application, we're not going to create a fancy model. The user we log in and out will just be the superuser created when we synchronize the database. So this example application is intended to run for only one user: the superuser (that is, you).

If you want, you can add other users to the application (as we did in Chapter 6), letting them log in and out too. To do that, edit models.py, which looks like this currently:

```
from django.db import models
# Create your models here.
Then add the User class to the model::
from django.db import models

from django.contrib.aut.models import
    User
```

After you synchronize the database (with `manage.py syncdb` as shown in the following task), you can add more users with the shell:

```
$python manage.py shell
>>> from login.models import *
>>> User.objects.create_user(
... username='nancy',
... email='nancy@nancy.com',
... password='opensesame'
... )
```

Alternatively, you can create new users in code:

```
from django.contrib.auth.models import
    User
User.objects.create_user(
username='nancy',
password='opensesame',
email='nancy@nancy.com'
)
```

```
DATABASE_ENGINE = ''          #
     'postgresql_psycopg2',
     'postgresql', 'mysql', 'sqlite3'
     or 'oracle'.
DATABASE_NAME = ''            # Or path
     to database file if using
     sqlite3.
DATABASE_USER = ''            # Not used
     with sqlite3.
DATABASE_PASSWORD = ''        # Not used
     with sqlite3.
```

Listing 10.3 The settings.py file.

```
DATABASE_ENGINE = 'sqlite3'         #
     'postgresql_psycopg2',
     'postgresql', 'mysql', 'sqlite3'
     or 'oracle'.
DATABASE_NAME = 'logindb'           #
     Or path
     to database file if using
     sqlite3.
DATABASE_USER = ''           # Not used
     with sqlite3.
DATABASE_PASSWORD = ''       # Not used
     with sqlite3.
```

Listing 10.4 The edited settings.py file.

To create the database:

1. Using a text-editing program, open chapter10\settings.py and find the database section (**Listing 10.3**).

2. Enter **'sqlite3'** for the DATABASE_ENGINE setting and **logindb** for the DATABASE_NAME setting (**Listing 10.4**).

3. Save settings.py.

4. Open a command prompt and in the chapter10 directory, enter this command to set up the database system:

   $ python manage.py syncdb

5. When prompted to create a superuser for the database, enter this data:

   You just installed Django's auth system, which means you don't have any superusers defined.

   Would you like to create one now? (yes/no):

   Enter **yes**.

   Username:

   Enter a name.

   E-mail address:

   Enter an email address.

   Password:

   Enter a password.

   Password (again):

   Enter the password again.

The database is now set up with one super-user, whom we will let log in and out of our application (to add more users, follow the directions at the beginning of this task).

CREATING THE DATABASE

181

Connecting the URLs

Now we'll connect the URLs we'll use in this application—for the main page, the login page, and the logout page—in urls.py.

We'll connect the default URL to the main_page view as we've done before:

```
from django.conf.urls.defaults import *
from login.views import *

urlpatterns = patterns('',
  (r'^$', main_page),
        .
        .
        .
```

However, we'll use a different approach to connect the login and logout URLs. We'll connect the login URL to a Django class, django.contrib.auth.views.login (and provide a template in a subdirectory named registration of our templates directory), and the logout page to a view named logout_page, which will just call the logout method. So urls.py ends up looking like this:

```
from django.conf.urls.defaults import *
from login.views import *

urlpatterns = patterns('',
  (r'^$', main_page),
  (r'^login/$', 'django.contrib.auth.
    views.login'),
  (r'^logout/$', logout_page),
)
```

To connect the URLs:

1. Using a text editor, create the document chapter10\urls.py and enter the code shown in **Listing 10.5** to connect the default URL to a view named main_page.

```
from django.conf.urls.defaults import *
from login.views import *

urlpatterns = patterns('',
  (r'^$', main_page),
        .
        .
```

Listing 10.5 Starting urlspy.

```
from django.conf.urls.defaults import *
from login.views import *

urlpatterns = patterns('',
  (r'^$', main_page),
  (r'^login/$', 'django.contrib.auth.views.
    login'),
)       .
        .
        .
```

Listing 10.6 Editing urls.py.

```
from django.conf.urls.defaults import *
from login.views import *

urlpatterns = patterns('',
  (r'^$', main_page),
  (r'^login/$', 'django.contrib.auth.views.
    login'),
  (r'^logout/$', logout_page),
)
```

Listing 10.7 Completing urls.py.

2. Add the code to connect URLs that end with /login to the Django `django.contrib.auth.views.login` class (**Listing 10.6**).

3. Add the code to connect pages with the URL /logout to the view logout_page (**Listing 10.7**).

4. Save urls.py.

✔ Tip

■ In Python, code indentation counts, so be sure to indent properly.

Creating the Main Page View

Next we'll create the main page view. This is the page that invites the user to log in or welcomes the user by name if the user is already logged in. It also displays a link to log in or log out as appropriate.

In fact, all the work of creating this page will be done by the main page template—in the view, we'll just pass to the main_page template the request object that was passed to us. That request object includes not only the normal request object we get from a browser trying to download a URL, but also the User object, and the main_page.html template checks user.username to see if the user is logged in.

So how do we pass the request object to the main_page.html template? We pass the name of the template we want to use to the render_to_response() function, and we pass it a Context object created from the request object with the RequestContext class:

```
def main_page(request):
  return render_to_response('main_page.
    html', RequestContext(request))
```

To create the main page view:

1. Using a text editor, edit chapter10\login\views.py, adding the code shown in **Listing 10.8** to import the classes we'll need.

2. Add the code to create a new function named main_page() (**Listing 10.9**).

3. Add the code to pass the request object to the main_page.html template (**Listing 10.10**).

4. Save views.py.

```
from django.template import RequestContext
from django.shortcuts import
    render_to_response

        .
        .
        .
```

Listing 10.8 The views.py file.

```
from django.template import RequestContext
from django.shortcuts import
    render_to_response


def main_page(request):
        .
        .
        .
```

Listing 10.9 Editing views.py.

```
from django.template import RequestContext
from django.shortcuts import
    render_to_response


def main_page(request):
    return render_to_response('main_page.
        html', RequestContext(request))
        .
        .
        .
```

Listing 10.10 The edited views.py file.

```
<html>
  <head>
    <title>{% block title %}{% endblock %}
        </title>
  </head>

  <body>
    <h1>{% block head %}{% endblock %}</h1>
    {% block content %}{% endblock %}
    <br>
    <br>
    <br>
        .
        .
        .

  </body>
</html>
```

Listing 10.11 The base.html file.

Creating the Base Template

The pages in this application share the same basic construction: a title, a header, some content, and links to the main page and the login and logout pages. For that reason, we'll create a base template and let the other templates inherit from it.

The base template will have a title, header, and body content just like the base template we created in Chapter 7, but it will also include code to check whether the user is logged in. If the user is logged in, the template will display a link to let the user log out, and if the user is not logged in, the template will display a link to let the user log in.

To create the base template:

1. Open a command prompt and change to the chapter10 directory:

   `$ cd \django-1.1\duango\bin\ chapter10`

2. Create a new directory to hold our templates, naming the directory templates:

   `$ md templates`

3. Using a text editor, create the template chapter10\templates\base.html and add the contents shown in **Listing 10.11** to display the title, header, and content.

   continues on next page

4. Add the code to add a link to the main page, check the user.is_authenticated value, and display the log in or log out link accordingly (**Listing 10.12**).

5. Save base.html.
   That completes the base template.

6. Add the new templates directory to the TEMPLATE_DIRS section of settings.py (**Listing 10.13**).

7. Save settings.py.

```html
<html>
  <head>
    <title>{% block title %}{% endblock %}
        </title>
  </head>

  <body>
    <h1>{% block head %}{% endblock %}</h1>
    {% block content %}{% endblock %}
    <br>
    <br>
    <br>
    <a href="/">Main page</a>
    {% if user.is_authenticated %}
      <a href="/logout/">Log out</a>
    {% else %}
      <a href="/login/">Log in</a>
    {% endif %}
  </body>
</html>
```

Listing 10.12 The completed base.html file.

```
TEMPLATE_DIRS = (
"C:/django/Django-1.1/django/bin/chapter10/
    templates"
)
```

Listing 10.13 The settings.py file.

```
{% extends "base.html" %}

{% block title %}Welcome User{% endblock %}
{% block head %}Welcome User{% endblock %}

{% block content %}
         .
         .
         .
{% endblock %}
```

Listing 10.14 The edited main_page.html file.

```
{% extends "base.html" %}

{% block title %}Welcome User{% endblock %}
{% block head %}Welcome User{% endblock %}

{% block content %}
  {% if user.username %}
    <p>Hello {{ user.username }}</p>
  {% else %}
    <p>Please <a href="/login">log in</a>.
  {% endif %}
{% endblock %}
```

Listing 10.15 The completed main_page.html file.

Creating the Main Page Template

In the main page template, we want to check whether the user is logged in. We can do that by checking user.username:

```
{% if user.username %}
     .
     .
     .
```

If the user is logged in, we can greet the user by name:

```
{% if user.username %}
  <p>Hello {{ user.username }}</p>
     .
     .
     .
```

Otherwise, we can invite the user to log in with a hyperlink to the login page:

```
{% if user.username %}
  <p>Hello {{ user.username }}</p>
{% else %}
  <p>Please <a href="/login">log
     in</a>.
{% endif %}
```

We'll create the main page template now, extending the base template to do that.

To create the main page template:

1. Using a text editor, create chapter10\
   templates\main_page.html and add
   the code in **Listing 10.14** to customize
   the blocks this template will inherit
   from the base template.

2. Add the code to welcome the user
   by name or invite the user to log in
   (**Listing 10.15**).

3. Save main_page.html.

Creating the Login Page Template

We've connected the login URL to the `django.contrib.auth.views.login` class in urls.py:

```
from django.conf.urls.defaults import *
from login.views import *
urlpatterns = patterns('',
  (r'^$', main_page),
  (r'^login/$', 'django.contrib.auth.
    views.login'),
)          .
             .
             .
```

This class looks for the template login.html in a subdirectory named registration within the templates directory. We'll create that template now.

To create the login page template:

1. Open a command prompt window and navigate to the chapter10/templates directory:

   `$ cd \django-1.1\duango\bin\`
      `chapter10\templates`

2. Create a new directory to hold our login template, naming the directory registration:

   `$ md registration`

3. Using a text editor, create chapter10\templates\registration\login.html and add the code in **Listing 10.16**.

   We'll start by checking whether an error occurred in an attempt to enter the password and username and, if so, display an error message.

```
{% extends "base.html" %}
{% block title %}Log in{% endblock %}
{% block head %}Log in{% endblock %}
{% block content %}
  {% if form.has_errors %}
    <p>Username or password didn't work.
        Please enter them again.</p>
  {% endif %}
          .
          .
          .
{% endblock %}
```

Listing 10.16 Creating login.html.

```
{% extends "base.html" %}
{% block title %}Log in{% endblock %}
{% block head %}Log in{% endblock %}
{% block content %}
  {% if form.has_errors %}
    <p>Username or password didn't work.
       Please enter them again.</p>
  {% endif %}

  <form method="post" action=".">
    <p><label for="id_username">Username:
       </label>{{ form.username }}</p>
    <p><label        .

               .

               .

  </form>
{% endblock %}
```

Listing 10.17 The edited login.html.

```
{% extends "base.html" %}
{% block title %}Log in{% endblock %}
{% block head %}Log in{% endblock %}
{% block content %}
  {% if form.has_errors %}
    <p>Username or password didn't work.
       Please enter them again.</p>
  {% endif %}
  <form method="post" action=".">
    <p><label for="id_username">Username:
       </label>{{ form.username }}</p>
    <p><label for="id_password">Password:
       </label>{{ form.password }}</p>
    <input type="hidden" name="next"
       value="/" />
    <input type="submit" value="Log in" />
  </form>
{% endblock %}
```

Listing 10.18 The completed login.html file.

4. Add the code for the HTML form that will display the username and password controls, including the code for the username control, which you reference as `form.username` (**Listing 10.17**).

5. Add the code to display the password control, the Log In button, and a hidden control indicating that the page displayed after a successful login should be the main page (**Listing 10.18**).

6. Save login.html.

CREATING THE LOGIN PAGE TEMPLATE

Creating the Logout View

Now we'll create the logout view that will log out the user. To do that, we only need to call the Django logout function and send the browser to the main page (which will invite the user to log in again).

To redirect the user to the main page, we'll use the Django function HttpResponseRedirect.

To create the logout view:

1. Using a text editor, edit chapter10\login\ views.py and add the code to create the logout view (**Listing 10.19**).

2. Add the code to log out the user and redirect the browser to the main page (**Listing 10.20**).

3. Save views.py.

```
from django.http import HttpResponse,
Http404, HttpResponseRedirect
from django.contrib.auth import logout
from django.contrib.auth.models import User
from django.template import RequestContext
from django.shortcuts import
    render_to_response


def main_page(request):
    return render_to_response('main_page.html',
        RequestContext(request))


def logout_page(request):
        .
        .
        .
```

Listing 10.19 Editing views.py.

```
from django.http import HttpResponse,
Http404, HttpResponseRedirect
from django.contrib.auth import logout
from django.contrib.auth.models import User
from django.template import RequestContext
from django.shortcuts import
    render_to_response


def main_page(request):
    return render_to_response('main_page.html',
        RequestContext(request))


def logout_page(request):
    logout(request)
    return HttpResponseRedirect('/')
```

Listing 10.20 The completed views.py file.

Logging In and Out

In this task, we'll test the login application, letting the user log in and out.

When the application first opens, it will display a page inviting the user to log in. When the user clicks a login link, the application will display the login page. After the user logs in, the user will be taken to the main page, which will welcome the user by name.

When the user is done, the user clicks the logout link, which returns the user to the main page, which invites the user to log in again.

Let's put the login application to the test now by running it.

To log in and out:

1. Open a command prompt window and navigate to the chapter10 directory:

```
$ cd django-1.1\django\bin\chapter10
```

2. Run the development server:

```
$ python manage.py runserver
```

3. Navigate your browser to http://localhost:8000.

You should see the Web page that appears in **Figure 10.1**. This is the main application page, and it invites you to log in.

continues on next page

Figure 10.1 The main page before you log in.

4. Click the Log In link.

The Log In page opens (**Figure 10.2**).

5. Enter your username.

6. Enter your password.

7. Click the Log In button.

The application logs you in and displays the main page, which greets you by name (**Figure 10.3**).

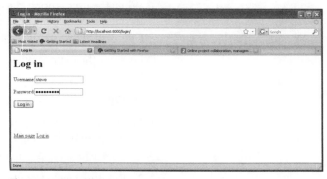

Figure 10.2 Logging in.

Figure 10.3 Greeting the logged-in user by name.

8. Click the Log Out link.

You'll be logged out, and the application will display the main page, which invites you to log in again (**Figure 10.4**).

Everything works as it should.

Figure 10.4 Inviting the logged-out user to log in.

INDEX

A

Accessing
  all user favorites, 76–77
  first favorite from model, 70–71
  specific user, 72–73
  specific user's favorite, 74–75
Application programming interface (API)
  connecting Django applications to, 16
  Linux systems, 5
Applications
  connecting view to model, 63–64
  creating favorites, 45
  Django. *See* Django applications
  login. *See* Login application
  multi-page. *See* multi-page applications
  for multi-page application, 84–85
Authorization, setting up database, 21

B

Base template
  changing, 133–135
  creating, 128, 185–186
  defined, 115–116
  inheriting, 129–132
  user template inheriting, 131–132
base.html
  changing base template, 133–134
  creating base template, 128, 185–186
  extending base template, 187–189
  inheriting base template, 129–131
Bindings, 17

<body>
  in base template, 133–134
  in style sheets, 108, 110
  in user template, 94, 126
  in Web pages, 101
built-in fields of User model, 55

C

Class(es)
  Django, 101, 109
  `django import forms`, 137
  `django.contrib.auth.views.login`,
    182–183, 188
  `django.views.static.serve`, 109
  `Hyperlink`, 48
  planning model, 46–47
  Python, 46
  `UserForm`, 142, 163, 167
`clean_item()` function, 157–159
`clean_password2()` function
  comparing passwords, 157–159
  validating password, 168
  validating username, 170
`clean_username()` function, 169–170
Collection command, in shell, 53
Commands. *See also specific commands*
  accessing in shell, 51
  in shell, 52–53
Compressed formats, 12
Context object.
  creating main view and, 120, 184
  data passed to template in, 36–37, 96, 97, 99

Index

W

Z